Slain Lamb

Standing

By Dana Kramer

Printed in the United States of America.

CONTENTS

INTRODUCTION

If we recognize Jesus as the *Lamb* of God who forgives and takes away our sins, why do we only put His blood on the doorposts of our lives to avoid the destroyer, yet neglect to eat (in haste) all the flesh of the *Lamb*? (Exodus 12:10-11; 23)

Manna rained down from heaven of which they were commanded not to leave any of it till morning. In other words, they were to consume it completely. Jesus compares Himself with this Manna: *"I am the living bread that came down from heaven!"* (Exodus 16:4, 19; John 6:51-53)

Jesus said we were to eat His flesh and drink His blood in order to have life. This statement was a major stumbling block to the Jews. He said the words that He spoke were spirit and life. If we believe Him why do we neglect to eat His flesh and drink His blood as Jesus told us to do? The results of neglecting this command will cause us to be just an empty shell with the label "Christian" on it. I see empty shells walking! (John 6:53)

The marriage will come! Has the *Lamb's* wife made herself ready? (Revelation 19:7)

THE NEW JERUSALEM
The *Lamb's* Wife

I saw no temple in it, for the Lord God Almighty and the "Lamb" are its temple. The "Lamb" is its light. There shall by no means enter it anything that defiles, or causes an abomination or a lie, but only those who are written in the "Lamb's" book of Life. (How much of the "Lamb" must we consume in order to be recorded in this book?) *He showed me a pure river of water of life, clear as crystal, proceeding from the throne of God and of the "Lamb". There shall be no more curse, but the throne of God and of the "Lamb" shall be in it, and His servants shall serve Him.* (Revelation 21-22)

---*Behold, I am coming quickly!*---

CHAPTER 1

WILL YOU RECOGNIZE HIM?

"THE REVELATION OF JESUS CHRIST WHICH
GOD GAVE HIM TO SHOW HIS SERVANTS . . ."
Revelation 1:1

We all want to believe that we are His servant, because we have been born again. Some will actually walk and talk as if having first class access to the throne room, but in reality are only seeing in a mirror dimly. John the Apostle walked with Jesus very closely for three years. Jesus invited John, James, and Peter to go with Him in situations where the others were left out. John knew Jesus and could recognize Him in a crowd. Jesus loved and trusted John and even entrusted His own mother into John's care. They knew each other very well. The Father also trusted John and put in his care the proclamation of the revelation of Jesus Christ as Revelation 1:1-11 indicates. If John knew Jesus so very well, why does he say in verses 12 and 13, *"I turned to see the voice that spoke with me. And having turned I saw . . . One **like** the Son of Man!"* (emphasis mine) It sounds as if John did not completely recognize Him. Then John, in terror, proclaims in verse 17, *"And when I saw Him, I fell at His feet as dead."* Why would John respond this way to a man he had walked with for three years, was entrusted with His mother, and knew how much he was loved by Him?

I have heard it said from many a saint that when they see Jesus in Eternity they will run up to Him and give Him a big hug or dance with Him hand in hand. Do they know something that John didn't know? Do they know Jesus better than John did? If John fell down as though dead . . . !?

Mary also knew Jesus and was outside the tomb after His death. Was Jesus' response to Mary indicating to her that she should not remember Him as He was because He had not yet ascended to His Father (John 20:16-17)? He had told her not to cling to Him. If John didn't quite recognize Him, neither would Mary.

The two disciples on the road to Emmaus didn't recognize Jesus after His resurrection. Jesus walked with them and ended up staying with them and wasn't recognized by them until He broke bread and gave them some. Then their eyes were opened and they realized their hearts had been burning all the while He spoke to them. They immediately returned to Jerusalem and told the others what had happened. As they spoke to them, Jesus simply appeared in their midst. It says they were terrified! They did not recognize Jesus! In fact, He had to eat a piece of fish in order to show them He wasn't a ghost.

In Revelation chapters 2 and 3, Jesus endeavors to reveal Himself in His eternal state to the seven churches. He addresses each church with the eternal aspect of His very description:

"These things says the Son of God, who has eyes like a flame of fire." (Revelation 2:18)

"These things says He who has the seven Spirits of God and the seven stars." (Revelation 3:1)

"These things says the Amen, the Faithful and True Witness, the Beginning of the creation of God." (Revelation 3:14)

He wanted each of His servants to realize that He was not just a man. He was the Alpha and Omega; the beginning and the end; the One who is and who was and who is to come; the Almighty (Revelation 1:8). If we truly have a revelation and understanding of who Jesus is, our response will be like the response of the twenty-four elders:

. . . the twenty-four elders fall down before Him . . .
(Revelation 4:10)

. . . the twenty-four elders fell down before the Lamb . . .
(Revelation 5:8)
. . . the twenty-four elders fell down and worshiped Him who lives forever and ever. (Revelation 5:14)

. . . All the angels stood around the throne and the elders and the four living creatures, and fell on their faces . . .
(Revelations 7:10-11)

Whenever they encountered the "Lamb" they didn't cheer, clap, shout or jump up and down. They fell! Within the book of Revelation, God endeavors to reveal Jesus the way that He saw Him; **A Lamb**!

A SCROLL, A SEALED BOOK IN HIS HAND
(Revelation 5:1)

A voice like a trumpet spoke with John saying, *"Come up here, and I will show you things which must take place after this."* John was caught up to heaven and saw revelations of the One who sat on the throne. His description, as John attempted to describe, is far beyond our imagination of what the Father actually looks like. We could be forever caught up in the wonder of that scene alone! John points out something that we might have missed as we gazed at this One on the throne. He says, *"I saw in the right hand of Him who sat on the throne a scroll written inside and on the back, sealed with seven seals."* (Revelation 5:1) The Father holding this scroll indicates that the content of it is of utmost importance. I must point out a Scripture that coincides with the scroll being written on both sides. *"And Moses turned and went down the mountain, and the two tablets of the **Testimony** were in His hand. The tablets **were written on both sides**; on the one side and on the other they were written. Now the tablets were the **work of God**, and the writing was **the writing of God** engraved on the tablets"* (Exodus 32:15-16 emphasis mine). From the very beginning God has desired to make known His mysteries. You will notice that these tablets were not called "Law" but "Testimony," even though the law was given at that time. They were the work of God expressing His very heart upon them. He is giving Moses instruction on the tabernacle set up for the purpose of dwelling with them. His desire is to dwell with us! You will notice in Genesis 24:12 and 31:18 something worth noting. *"Then the Lord said to Moses, 'Come up to Me on the mountain and be there; and **I will give you** tablets of stone, and the law and commandments which I have written."* *"And when He had made an end of speaking with him on Mount Sinai, **He gave Moses two tablets of the Testimony**, tablets of stone, written with the finger of God."* (emphasis mine) These tablets, written on both sides, were given by God to Moses. These tablets were given at the same time that God gave instructions to Moses on the tabernacle to make it just like the one in heaven. Coincidence? I'm sure John was aware of these passages in Genesis. John not only sees the scroll in the right hand of Him who sits on the throne, but he also sees that the scroll has not just three or four seals, but seven seals on it. The intent of pointing this out is not to analyze the number seven and if it has some significant meaning. This observation by John is to point out that the scroll was "sealed shut" and could not be opened.

WHAT DID JOHN SEE --- LION OR LAMB?

At this point, a strong angel proclaiming with a **loud** voice (emphasis on loud for the soft spoken), *"Who is worthy to open the scroll and to loose its seals?"* Or as Amplified writes, *"Who is worthy . . . to break its seals?"* (I will talk more about the breaking

13

of the seals in the next chapter.) John observes that no one stepped
forward or was indicated to open the scroll, or to look at it. John
could have considered himself as a possibility. He had walked with
Jesus and had become a close friend and comrade, yet was coming to
the conclusion very quickly that he and no one else was worthy. All
of heaven and earth and those under the earth couldn't even look at
it! John was overcome with weeping; much weeping! He knew the
importance of breaking these seals in order to reveal what the Father
had written on it. If what is written on the scroll is the same as what
was written on the tablets, then it also refers to the Testimony and
the Law of God. The Testimony is God testifying about Himself;
who He is and what He is like, and His Law which refers to quality
of life in His kingdom. John had heard Jesus testify concerning all
the wonderful things about the Father and His kingdom. He had
seen the Father in Jesus as He walked among the people. Some of
the things that could of went through John's mind at this time could
be taken from his gospel. He had written about many things that he
had seen Jesus do: the miraculous healings, multitudes fed because
of compassion, the wonder of walking on the sea, extreme
wickedness forgiven as with the woman caught in adultery, and
those who had never seen the light of day instantly receiving sight.
He had even seen the tremendous sorrow of close friends who had
lost their brother to death and then had seen death defeated because
of resurrection. John knew of God's tremendous goodness, mercy,
and love; and yet it looked as though all hope was lost in ever seeing
the fullness of it. But right at that moment one of the twenty-four
elders speaks to John, *"Do not weep. Behold, the Lion of the tribe of
Judah, the Root of David, has prevailed to open the scroll and (to
break) its seven seals."* (Revelation 5:5 - AMP) At this point, you
expect to see someone come riding in as described in Revelation
19:11; *"Now I saw heaven opened, and behold a white horse. And
He who sat on him was called Faithful and True."* But that is not
what John saw. He says, *"I looked, and behold, in the midst of the
throne and of the four living creatures, and in the midst of the elders,
stood a **Lamb** as though it had been **slain"** (Revelation 5:6 - emphasis
mine). He was seeing a young sheep slain, yet standing! Wow! He
not only saw this *Lamb,* but he saw that it had seven horns and seven
eyes! What a strange sight that must have been. Yet, John, not
being moved by this sight goes on to explain the seven eyes and

14

what the *Lamb* proceeded to do. The *Lamb* walked right up to the
One who sat on the throne and took the scroll out of His right hand.
I must emphasize something at this point. Revelation 1:1 says, *"The
revelation of Jesus Christ . . . to show His servants!"* Many would
say right here, "Dah, The *Lamb* is Jesus Christ!" Yes He is, but John
knew this as well. From the time of John the Baptist proclaiming
Jesus as the *Lamb* of God who takes away the sin of the world (John
1:29), John knew that Jesus was this *Lamb*. Most fathers would
display their son for all to see in greatness and in the finest clothing
and apparel. God chose to display His Son as a *Lamb,* slaughtered
by others. And thus, throughout the book of Revelation, the word
Lamb is mentioned twenty-five times. God chose to reveal His Son
in this way. Just a note: for those of us who have this concept of
marrying Jesus as His bride and sitting at table with Him at the
wedding supper; it must be known that Revelation 19:7 and 9 says,
"The marriage of the Lamb has come" and *"Blessed are those who
are called to the marriage supper of the Lamb!"* Yes Jesus is the
Lamb, but God describes this event as the *Lamb* being joined in
marriage to His bride. **The *Lamb* slain and standing with seven
horns and seven eyes**. This is the *Lamb* that we are to marry. The
angel in Revelation 21:9 speaks to John and says, *"Come, I will show
you the bride, the Lamb's wife."* Why didn't he say, "Come, I will
show you the bride, Jesus Christ's wife?" We, who are Gentiles, fail
to understand the importance of the slaughtered lamb for sin. It
dates all the way back to Abraham. God provided a lamb in Isaac's
place. Isaac was redeemed by a lamb. All of Israel was redeemed
from the death angel in Egypt by a lamb (Exodus 12). *"Your lamb
shall be without blemish, a male of the first year . . . kill it at
twilight. They shall take some of the blood and put it on the two
doorposts. The blood shall be a sign for you on the houses where
you are. And when I see the blood, I will pass over you"* (Exodus
12:5-7 and 13). Every first born son that was born was redeemed by a
lamb. (Exodus 13:13) When God promised to dwell among the
children of Israel and be their God, a sacrifice of two lambs per day
was to be offered at the tabernacle of meeting. One was offered in
the morning and the other was offered at twilight. (Exodus 29:38-46)
God's very presence dwelt within the tabernacle of meeting. This
was protocol for entering into God's presence from the beginning.

15

THE LAMB SLAUGHTERED STANDING

I must point out other very important Scriptures in regard to the *Lamb*. Revelation 14:1 says, *"Then I looked, and behold, a Lamb standing on Mount Zion, and with Him 144,000 having His Father's name **written on their foreheads."** (emphasis mine) This which is written on their forehead is in direct contrast to what was previously described in chapter 13:16-17 which says, *"He (the beast) causes all . . . to receive a mark on their right hand or **forehead."*** (emphasis mine) There will come more of a divide between light and darkness; between the holy and the unholy. In these last days it will become more evident who belongs to God and who doesn't. The evidence will be most obvious on their faces; even the faces of disobedient, lawless believers! When a teenager disobeys his parents, becomes rebellious against them, and then lies to them that he has been obedient; the obvious is on the face of the teenager that he is not speaking the truth. Attached to the rebellion and lies is a face that is undeniably full of shame. So it is with the disobedient and lawless. It goes on to say in chapter 14:9-10 that if anyone worships the beast, he will be tormented with fire and brimstone in the presence of the holy angels and in the presence of the *Lamb*. Chapter 15:1-3 describes those who are standing on the sea of glass mingled with fire as those who have victory over the beast. They are singing a song. The song of Moses and the song of the *Lamb*. We know the song of Moses because it's recorded in Deuteronomy 32, but who can sing to me the song of the *Lamb?* This song can only be sung by those who completely belong to Him! Again in Revelation 17:14 which states concerning the ten horns on the beast, *"These will make war with the Lamb, and the Lamb will overcome them."* The *Lamb* will overcome the ten horns or kings that are joined with the beast (Revelation 17:12). (The beast and the horns are expounded on in my first book, *The Counterfeit Woman*.) We can see in these Scriptures the importance of being rightly connected with the *Lamb*. There is no ability to overcome or have victory in the last of days unless we are completely and rightly connected with the *Lamb* of God who takes away our sin. Jesus proclaims to those in Matthew 7:21-23, who prophesy and do wonders in His name, that He never knew them because they practice lawlessness. They did not discern God's provision for sin and they were not rightly connected with the *Lamb*! It must be noticed that the word *Lamb* is used throughout the book of Revelation. His name, Jesus Christ, could have been used in all of these references, but God is drawing attention to relationship with the *Lamb* and He's doing it very intentionally. We must take notice!

Revelation 21 and 22 speaks of the holy city, New Jerusalem, descending out of heaven from God. Revelation 21:22-23 says, *"I saw no temple in it, for the Lord God Almighty and the Lamb are its temple. The city had no need of the sun or of the moon to shine in it, for the glory of God illuminated it. The Lamb is its light."* Remember the *Lamb* described here is the *Lamb* described in Revelation 5:6. We must be rightly related to God's provision! Revelation 21:27 and 22:15 (AMP) warn us of how important this is! *"Nothing that defiles or profanes or is unwashed shall ever enter it, nor anyone who commits abominations (unclean, detestable, morally repugnant things) or practices falsehood, but only those whose names are recorded in the Lamb's Book of Life." "Outside (the city) are dogs and sorcerers and sexually immoral and murderers and idolaters, and whoever loves and practices a lie."* Beloved, what is described in these verses is forever! We could quote the greatest commandment this way: *"You shall love the **Lamb** with all your heart, with all your soul, and with all your mind"* (Deuteronomy 6:5 - emphasis mine).

In Revelation 7:9, John sees a great multitude which no one could number. They are standing before the throne and before the *Lamb*. They are clothed in white and have palm branches in their hands. Verse 14 goes on to describe these as those who come out of the great tribulation. They are before the throne and serving God because they have washed their robes and made them white in the blood of the *Lamb*! They will not hunger or thirst anymore. The sun will not strike them, nor any heat, for the *Lamb* (described in Revelation 5:6) will shepherd them and lead them to living fountains of waters. They live in God forever because they have *"washed their robes in the blood of the Lamb!"* (Revelation 7:13) No stains or spots on their garments. They took great care to make sure their robes were clean when they anticipated standing before the throne of the King! We, in this day and age are very careless in keeping our robes clean! We must take the sacrifice of the lamb/*Lamb* seriously. *"Let us consider one another in order to stir up love and good works . . . exhorting one another, and so much the more as you see the day approaching. For if we sin willfully* (lawlessly) *after we have received the knowledge of the truth, there no longer remains a sacrifice for sin."* (Hebrews 10:24-29) We will trample the Son of God underfoot and count the blood of the covenant . . . a common thing and insult the Spirit of grace. When Jesus ascended to heaven (Acts 1:9-11), He presented Himself before the Father as the *Lamb* who takes away the sin of the world. I love what TD Jakes said in one of his sermons, "There is forever wet blood on the golden altar which is in heaven!" It forever speaks and cries out forgiveness and mercy towards us! What we do with it is our own choice. I will end this chapter with Isaiah 53:6-7: *All we like sheep have gone astray; we have turned, every one, to his own way; and the Lord has laid on Him* (the Lamb) *the iniquity* (lawlessness) *of us all. He was oppressed and He was afflicted, yet He opened not His mouth; He was led as a lamb to the slaughter, and as a sheep before its shearers is silent, so He opened not His mouth."*

Worthy is the *Lamb* that was slain to take the scroll, and to break open the seals!

CONSIDER THIS:

"The earth was without form, and void; and darkness was on the face of the deep. And the Spirit of God was hovering over the face of the waters. Then God said, 'Let there be light'; and there was light. And God saw the light, that it was good; and God divided the light from the darkness. God called the light Day, and the darkness He called Night.'" Genesis 1:2-5

In this day and age, the saying would be true; "We love the Night because we have created our own light!"

The earth is 6,000 to 7,000 years old. In the past 100 years or less, we have created our own light "throughout the earth" to rule the night. Call it creativity or ingenuity; I see electricity as mans own answer endeavoring to eradicate darkness. God's city is illuminated with the light of the *Lamb! "Your word is a lamp unto my feet and a light unto my path."* (Psalms 119:105)

SOMETHINGS UP! SOMETHINGS ABOUT TO HAPPEN!

CHAPTER 2

BREAK THE SEALS

THE SCROLL NEEDS TO BE OPENED!

Father, I ask You for clarity of speech and the touch of
Holy Spirit to be able to communicate what I have
received within the next few chapters of this book. I
understand the importance of rightly representing
Your Word. Help me to articulate with words as I
present Your Revelation and the unfolding of truth
within this book. Amen!

What I will present within the next chapters is only a
snapshot of all that God has to reveal concerning His mysteries.
God reveals His truth to many of His servants. He does not hide it
forever as Jesus proclaimed in Mark 4:22: *"For there is nothing*

hidden which will not be revealed, nor has anything been kept secret but that it should come to light." This Scripture is in the context of having good soil, hearing the word, accepting it, and bearing fruit. Mark 4:24-25 follows, *"Take heed what you hear. With the same measure you use, it will be measured to you; and to you who hear, more will be given."* Jesus was saying if any one has good soil, he will hear the hidden things of God and they will come to light. But this one must take heed and give himself to daily and actively pursuing the knowledge of the Lord; because in that pursuit, more will be given. Everyone that names His Name in servanthood to Him will be encountered by God the Father face to face. There are many pieces of the puzzle held by many saints and all the pieces will present the whole picture as God unfolds His mysteries.

> *" I saw as the Lamb broke open one of the seven seals, and as if in a voice of thunder I heard one of the four living creatures call out, Come!"* (Revelation 6:1-2 - AMP).

We must understand that these seals keep the scroll from being opened. They must be broken off in order for the scroll to be read. I compare this to a sealed envelope that you have just put a birthday card in and you forgot to put money in the card. You now have a problem. How do I open the envelope in order to put the money in? At this point the emphasis is not on the card but the seal that must be opened. The same would be with a cereal box. In order to have a bowl of cereal, you must break open the seal on the top of the box in order to release the contents. Again the emphasis is on the seal being broken in order to have your cereal. The seal has nothing to do with what is inside the box, but has everything to do with keeping it sealed shut. As this chapter unfolds, we will see that these seals are not judgments released into the earth, but established hindrances to the opening of the glorious writings of God that are on the scroll. The first four seals are presented as horses with riders upon them. As we look at the first four seals, we must begin by observing what Scripture says about horses and the significance of horses at that period of time.

HORSES OR SPIRITS?

Jeremiah was prophesying to Israel and proclaiming that because of her harlotry against the Lord, He was sending Babylon against them. Jeremiah is descriptive when he speaks of judgment and Babylon's horses: *"The snorting of [Nebuchadnezzar's] horses is heard from Dan [on the northern border of Palestine]. At the sound of the neighing of his strong war-horses the whole land quakes; for they come and devour the land and all that is in it, the city and those who dwell in it."* (Jeremiah 8:16 - AMP) There is something presented here that goes far beyond ordinary horses. Just the sound of them produces terror. Again in Jeremiah 47:1-3, he is descriptive as he speaks of judgment on the Philistines: *"The word of the Lord that came to Jeremiah the prophet against the Philistines, before Pharaoh attacked Gaza. Thus says the Lord: 'Behold, waters rise out of the north, and shall be an overflowing flood; they shall overflow the land and all that is in it, the city and those who dwell within; then the men shall cry, and all the inhabitants of the land shall wail. At the noise of the stamping hooves of his strong horses, at the rushing of his chariots."* Here it says that men will cry and wail at the sound of their stamping hooves. They are described as an overflowing flood. There are many other Scriptures such as these which are descriptive about horses as well. I will point out two more before continuing. Zechariah speaks of horses in chapters one and six. He speaks of them as spirits of judgment. *"I saw by night, and behold, a man riding on a red horse, and it stood among the myrtle trees in the hollow; and behind him were horses: red, sorrel, and white. Then I said, 'My Lord, what are these?' So the angel who talked with me said to me, 'I will show you what they are.' And the man who stood among the myrtle trees answered and said, 'These are the ones whom the Lord has sent to walk to and fro throughout the earth.'"* (Zechariah 1:8-10) Zechariah 6:5 says of these horses: *"These are four spirits of heaven, who go out from their station before the Lord of all the earth."* Zechariah 1:12 explains why the Lord sent these horses: *"Then the Angel of the Lord answered and said, 'O Lord of hosts, how long will You not have mercy on Jerusalem and on the cities of Judah, against which You were angry these seventy years?'"* The horses were sent spirits of judgment against Jerusalem and the cities of Judah. We know from Scripture that Babylon came and utterly destroyed Jerusalem and the temple. Many people were slaughtered and also carried away as captives to Babylon. Young men were castrated and made slaves as Daniel mentions in chapter 1:3 of his book. Zechariah 6 speaks of horses again in a vision. What precedes this vision in chapter 6, of four chariots and horses as spirits that go out from the Lord, is important to point out. Chapter 5 mentions a flying scroll with a curse against every thief and the one who swears falsely by God's name. Right after the vision of the scroll an angel shows him another vision which is connected to the first one. He sees a basket that is presented. Zechariah 5:6 (AMP) explains: *"This that goes forth is an ephah [sized vessel for separate grains all collected together]. This, he continued, is the symbol of the sinners mentioned above and is the resemblance of their iniquity throughout the whole land."* Their resemblance: A woman representing wickedness sitting inside the basket! (Zechariah 5:7-8) The wickedness: Thieves and perjurers (the ones who swear falsely by My name)! Note: Jesus describes a thief in Matthew 21:12-13; *"Then Jesus went into the temple of God and drove out all those who bought and sold in the temple, and overturned the tables of the money changers and the seats of those who sold doves. And He said to them, 'It is written, My house shall be called a house of prayer, but you have made it a den of thieves.'"* He was calling these merchandisers thieves. These along with the religious leaders were perjurers. They did not rightly represent the Lord. They were concerned about making money and not the hearts of those who were offering the sacrifices. Continuing with Zechariah's vision: Two women with wings like storks lifted up the basket and Zechariah asks, *"'Where are they carrying the basket?' And he said to me, 'To build a house for it in the land of Shinar, when it is ready, the basket will be set there on its base.'"* (Zechariah 5:10-11) The land of Shinar is modern day Iraq and is where Babylon was. Are we seeing (before our very eyes) the house being built for the basket of wickedness to be set there on its base? At present, ISIS has taken over many cities in Iraq. They are threatening the entire world, especially the western nations. They are beheading captives while video taping them. These videos are being presented by news agencies for all the world to see.

So we see that immediately after the vision of the basket, Zechariah sees four chariots coming from between two mountains of bronze. (Zechariah 6:1-7) The chariots had horses: red, black, white and dappled---strong steeds. The angel who was talking with him goes on to explain these horses. *" 'These are four spirits of heaven, who go out from their station before the Lord of all the earth.' Then the strong steeds went out, eager to go, that they might walk to and fro throughout the earth."* Again these are spirits of judgment sent out into the earth as the angel describes to Zechariah in 6:8 (AMP), *"Then He summoned me and said to me, 'Behold, these that go toward the north country have quieted My Spirit [of wrath] and have caused it to rest in the north country.' "* God had caused His Spirit of wrath to rest in that country because the white horses went there. The point is that the horses represent God's wrath upon Israel. God used Babylon and showed His prophet, Zechariah, horses of judgment.

We see in Revelation 6:2-8 that there are four horses described as spirits of judgment. Coincidence? The judgments that proceed from these horses and their riders has already been established in the earth. What happened with Babylon has been remembered through history. Israel was never the same.

THE FIRST SEAL BROKEN
"I looked, and behold, a white horse . . ."
Revelation 6:2

The first seal broken off the scroll is a white horse and rider with a bow, a crown, and going forth conquering and to conquer. One of the first Scriptures that talks about a bow is in II Kings 13:14-19 which says, *"Joash the king of Israel came down to him* (Elisha) *and said, 'O my father, my father, the chariots of Israel and their horsemen!' And Elisha said to him, 'Take a bow and some arrows.' So he took himself a bow and some arrows. Then he said to the king of Israel, 'Put your hand on the bow.' So he put his hand on it, and Elisha put his hands on the king's hands. And he said, 'Open the east window'; and he opened it. Then Elisha said, 'Shoot'; and he shot. And he said, 'The arrow of the Lord's deliverance and the arrow of deliverance from Syria; for you must strike the Syrians at Aphek till you have destroyed them.' "* The Lord's purposes for Israel was to completely conquer Syria. Elisha's hands on the king's hands, which were on the bow, were a sign of God's power being with Israel to enable them to completely conquer Syria. In 1 Samuel 18:4, Jonathan, who was set to be king after his father Saul, gave David his bow along with his robe, armor, and belt. He knew David would be the next king and was proclaiming David as a conqueror. These Scriptures mentioned were situations in which conquering was accomplished for the good. Many other Scriptures throughout the Old Testament, which I will not go into, mention the bow (and horses) in a destructive way. The bow was always mentioned in conjunction with conquering the enemy or another nation. We can see this conquering mentality as far back as Genesis 14:1-17, where several kings attacked other kings, one being Sodom were Lot lived. Again the motive was to conquer. I will let you read the rest of the story yourself. We can see that this was already in the earth and is not a judgment that is released when the seal is broken off the scroll. I cannot emphasize this enough. Beloved, if Daniel's den of lions had a seal on it so it couldn't be opened . . . Daniel 6:17; if Jesus' tomb had a seal on it so it couldn't be opened . . . Matthew 27:66; if Satan had a seal put on him for a thousand years so he couldn't deceive the nations . . . Revelation 20:2-3; if the vision in Isaiah's day had become like a book that was sealed so it couldn't be opened and read . . . Isaiah 29:11; and if the words of the vision revealed to Daniel were closed and shut up and sealed so no one could understand until the time of the end . . . Daniel 12:4,9; then the seals that are on the scroll will keep the content of the scroll from being read and released. Each one of the seals must be individually broken off in order for the *Lamb* to open and read the scroll.

THE SECOND SEAL BROKEN
"Another horse, fiery red, went out"
Revelation 6:4.

The second seal broken off the scroll is a fiery red horse with rider who takes peace from the earth so that men slaughter one another; he was given a huge sword. This looks so very much like Satan himself. From Cain, who slaughtered Abel, this very thing has dominated the entire earth. Men have been slaughtering one another since the beginning. An example from the past would be the Nazi concentration camps and the slaughter of millions of Jews. Was Babylon's invasion of Israel and Jerusalem in Jeremiah's day any different? When has there not been a mass slaughtering of people in the earth? The statement *"he was given a great sword"* (Revelation 6:4) has to be looked at with a question, "Who gave him (or allowed him to have) the great sword?"

The first mention of sword in the Bible is Genesis 3:24, *He drove out the man and He placed cherubim at the east of the garden of Eden, and a flaming sword which turned every way, to guard the way to the tree of life."* The sword was a weapon to keep the man from partaking of the tree of life. Then the man Adam knew his wife Eve and she conceived a son and named him Cain. Cain slaughtered Abel and then went out from the presence of the Lord. (Genesis 4:16) Cain's great, great, great grandson was Lamech, a man with an attitude, (read Genesis 4:23-24). Lamech married two wives. The second wife Zillah had a son who was named Tubal-cain. Genesis 4:22 (AMP) says, *He* (Tubal-cain) *was the forger of all [cutting] instruments of bronze and iron.* New King James Version says, "*He was an instructor of every craftsman in bronze and iron."* Tubal-cain was an instructor and maker of swords. Remember, Cain went out from the presence of the Lord. All his relatives did not walk in the presence of the Lord. Then after a few years Genesis 6:5 says, "*Then the Lord saw that the wickedness of man was great on the earth, and that every intent of the thoughts of his heart was only evil continually."* And then in Genesis 6:11 it says, "*The earth also was corrupt before God, and the earth was filled with violence."* This Scripture indicates that the earth also was filled with violence just as man was. This is only assumption because of the way it is worded in Scripture, but it sounds like they were killing one another at that time. Lamech mentions that he killed two men and was going to be avenged for it. (Genesis 4:23) The word sword is mentioned in the Old Testament 387 times. It is most often mentioned in the context of killing or being killed. The Lord through Isaiah speaks to Israel in Isaiah 1:19-20, "*If you are willing and obedient, you shall eat the good of the land; but if you refuse and rebel, you shall be devoured by the sword."* Throughout Scripture, enemies were raised up against Israel when she was disobedient and rebellious. The result of this disobedience and rebellion was that Israel was slaughtered by the sword when wicked nations came against her. Wicked nations were also slaughtered by the sword. Of Egypt it says, *"This is the day of the Lord God of hosts, a day of vengeance, that He may avenge Himself on His adversaries. The sword shall devour; It shall be satiated and made drunk with their blood."* Of Babylon it says, *" 'A sword is against the Chaldeans,' says the Lord, 'against the inhabitants of Babylon, and against her princes and her wise men. A sword is against the soothsayers, and they will be fools. A sword is against her mighty men, and they will be dismayed. A sword is against their horses, against their chariots, and against all the mixed peoples who are in her midst.' "* The sword has always threatened or killed from the beginning. So again, the seal must be broken off of the scroll. Only the *Lamb* is worthy to do this.

You will notice that with the second rider *"**it was granted** to take peace and that men would slaughter one another."* (emphasis mine) Who granted this? Make sure you are in correct, intimate relationship with God the Father before you even begin to endeavor to answer this question!

CHAPTER 3

THE SEALS NEED TO BE BROKEN OFF

THE THIRD SEAL BROKEN
"A black horse . . . he who sat on it had a pair of scales in his hand."
Revelation 6:5

The third seal broken off the scroll is a black horse with rider who had a pair of scales in his hand. What is different about this seal is that the rider was not given or granted anything like with the other three riders, but was given a command. A voice in the midst of the four living creatures spoke! John's description of the throne in Revelation 4:5 mentions voices coming from the throne: *"And from the throne proceeded lightnings, thunderings, and voices."* The Father is giving a command to this rider, just as He gave a command to Satan concerning Job: *"Behold, all that he has is in your power; only do not lay a hand on his person."* (Job 1:12) The command to the rider: *"A quart of wheat for a denarius, and three quarts of barley for a denarius; and do not harm the oil and the wine."* A denarius would be the equivalent of a day's wage for a laborer. This seems to be mercy when you look at the story in 2 Kings 6:24-7:1. Syria had besieged Samaria. The definition of besiege is to surround, crowd around or overwhelm; as a castle is surrounded by armed forces. Because of this, there was a great famine in Samaria. II Kings 6:25 describes how bad it was: *"A donkey's head was sold for eighty shekels of silver* (320 day's wages), *and one-fourth of a kab* (one pint) *of dove droppings for five shekels of silver* (20 day's wages)."* It was a very desperate situation in Samaria; to the point that they were eating their own children (2 Kings 6:28-29). The point of mentioning these Scriptures is not to highlight how bad it gets. I mention them only to point out that this seal is not a judgment released into the earth, but something that needs to be broken off the scroll. God's mercy was manifested in the middle of this famine. Elisha prophesied in 2 Kings 7: 1 saying, *"Thus says the Lord: Tomorrow about this time a seah* (7 quarts) *of fine flour shall be sold for a shekel* (4 day's wages), *and two seahs of barley for a shekel, at the gate of Samaria."* Syria had fled because they heard the sound of horses, chariots, and a great army and left all their stuff! I would say that was God's mercy. So, even though there will be judgments on the earth in the last days, we can trust God for His provision at all times.

"DO NOT HARM THE OIL AND THE WINE"

There was the command given to not harm the oil and the wine. God sets things apart for His purposes and declares them holy. He did this for His own Son thousands of years before Jesus was even born. In Exodus 13:13, *"Every firstborn of a donkey you shall redeem with a lamb; and if you will not redeem it, then you shall break its neck."* Is God cruel, or is He setting this animal apart for what is to come in the future? Zechariah 9:9/Matthew 21:5 proclaims, *"Behold, your King is coming to you, lowly, and sitting on a donkey, a colt, the foal of a donkey."* Is that cool or what?

THE WINE!

Just a note to all the wine drinkers, beer guzzlers, and residents of margaritaville: This is not a justification for drinking! Scripture is very clear on this subject and to reference them all would be a rabbit trail, so I will refrain. I know its a hot button for some, but we must study and discover what God really thinks about this subject. Many argue that the drinking of wine is mentioned throughout the Bible, but we must ask, "What was the wine; crushed grapes made into juice or fermented alcoholic beverage?" The Scriptures in Jeremiah's day would give some light on this subject. Lamentations 2 talks of the days of Babylon's siege against Jerusalem and mentions what the children were saying to their mothers during this siege. They were asking in verse 12, *"Where is the grain and wine?"* Children would not be asking for fermented wine in the midst of starvation. We must rethink the definition of wine in the Scriptures and stop justifying our drunkenness of one glass or four! Sorry for the bluntness. There is too much compromise in God's people! He wants disciples, not drunken or even buzzed up followers.

The first mention of wine in the Scriptures was in Genesis 14:18 when Melchizedek met with Abram (or Abraham) and blessed him. This was a very holy moment for Abraham because as Hebrews 7:1-3 says concerning Melchizedek, *"For this Melchizedek, king of Salem, priest of the Most High God . . . King of Salem (*king of peace)*, without father, without mother, without genealogy, having neither beginning of days nor end of life, but made like the Son of God, remains a priest continually."* Melchizedek brought the wine and bread and blessed Abraham. The Son of God also ate the Passover with His disciples having bread and wine and blessed His followers. This was a holy moment. The priest of the God of the universe (Melchizedek) was meeting with Abraham face to face in the secret place. They were having fellowship together. Again in Exodus 29:37-41, the Lord gives instructions to Moses: *"Seven days you shall make atonement for the altar and sanctify it. The altar shall be most holy. Whatever touches the altar must be holy. Now this is what you shall offer on the altar: two lambs of the first year,* *day by day continually. One lamb you shall offer in the morning, and the other lamb you shall offer at twilight. With the one lamb shall be one-tenth of an ephah of flour mixed with one-fourth of a hin of pressed oil, and one-fourth of a hin of wine as a drink offering."* This mixture of wine was for a drink offering. It was holy, set apart for the Lord. Whatever touches the altar must be holy! In the beginning, wine was set apart unto God for holy purposes. In Isaiah 5, it speaks of a vineyard. It's not just any vineyard; Isaiah speaks of his "Well-Beloved's" vineyard: *"Now let me sing to my Well-Beloved a song of my Beloved regarding His vineyard. My Well-Beloved has a vineyard on a very fruitful hill. He dug it up and cleared out its stones, and planted it with the choicest vine. He built a tower in its midst, and also made a winepress in it; So He expected it to bring forth good grapes, but it brought forth wild grapes"* (verses 1-2). In verse 7, he explains that the vineyard is the house of Israel. Since Jesus' dad was God the Father, it is no coincidence that Jesus also talked about a vineyard. In Matthew 20:1-15, Jesus gives a parable concerning his workers in His vineyard. Again in Matthew 21:33-41, He speaks concerning His vineyard and the vinedressers of that vineyard. The vinedressers were wicked and wanted the vineyard for themselves so they killed the landowner's son in order to keep it for themselves. In both parables it was all about the vineyard. It was God's vineyard where He desired to have sweet fellowship with the people who would love Him extremely well. The laborers (Apostles, Prophets, Evangelists, Pastors and Teachers) or anyone who worked in the vineyard long hours complained because it was hard work bringing forth the fruit of the vine. They didn't think it was fair for those who worked just a little to be paid the same as they were. Again, it was all about the vineyard and receiving the fruit of the vine from it. In Matthew 26:29, Jesus makes a statement that I have never understood until I began to write this section. He says to His disciples after He had given them the bread and wine during the last supper: *"I say to you, I will not drink of this fruit of the vine from now on until that day when I drink it new with you in My Father's kingdom."* When Jesus returns and claims His people, it is then that He will participate of the fruit of His vineyard (sweet fellowship with His people forever)! Thus the command was given to the rider of the black horse: "Do not harm the wine!"

THE OIL!

The first mention of oil in Scripture was in Exodus 25:1-6. *"Then the Lord spoke to Moses, saying: 'Speak to the children of Israel, that they bring Me an offering. From everyone who gives it willingly with his heart you shall take My offering. And this is the offering which you shall take from them: . . . oil for the light, and spices for the anointing oil.' "* Also in Exodus 29:7, *"And you shall take the anointing oil, and pour it on his head, and anoint him."* Aaron was anointed to be priest in the tabernacle. The tabernacle and all of that which was within the tabernacle was also to be anointed. Exodus 30:22-33 says, *"The Lord spoke to Moses, saying: 'Also take for yourself quality spices---five hundred shekels of liquid myrrh, half as much sweet-smelling cinnamon, two hundred and fifty shekels of sweet-smelling cane, five hundred shekels of cassia, according to the shekel of the sanctuary, and a hin of olive oil. And you shall make from these a holy anointing oil, an ointment compounded according to the art of the perfumer. It shall be a holy anointing oil. With it you shall anoint the tabernacle of meeting and the ark of the Testimony; the table and all its utensils, the lampstand and its utensils, and the altar of incense; the altar of burnt offering with all its utensils, and the laver and its base. You shall consecrate them, that they may be most holy; whatever touches them must be holy.' "* Take notice of what the Lord says in verses 31-33, *"This shall be a holy anointing oil to Me throughout your generations. It shall not be poured on man's flesh; nor shall you make any other like it, according to its composition. It is holy, and it shall be holy to you. Whoever compounds any like it, or whoever puts any of it on an outsider, shall be cut off from his people."* This tabernacle which was the meeting place between God and man was to be kept holy. We enter God's presence so lightly sometimes. We are full of the world and distracted when we come to God and we must be washed and cleansed before we can meet with Him in the secret place. Matthew 25:1-13 is a parable concerning the holy anointing oil and meeting with God in the secret place. We know it as the parable of the ten virgins. *"Then the kingdom of heaven shall be likened to ten virgins who took their lamps and went out to meet the bridegroom. Those who were foolish took their lamps and took no oil with them, but the wise took oil in their vessels with their lamps. While the bridegroom was delayed, they all slumbered and slept. And at midnight a cry* (or trumpet) *was heard: 'Behold, the bridegroom is coming; go out to meet him!' Then all those virgins arose and trimmed their lamps. And the foolish said to the wise, 'Give us some of your oil, for our lamps are going out.' But the wise answered, saying, 'No, lest there should not be enough for us and you; but go rather to those who sell, and buy for yourselves.' And while they went to buy, the bridegroom came, and those who were ready went in with him to the wedding;* **and the door was shut.** *Afterward the other virgins came also, saying, 'Lord, Lord, open to us!' But He answered and said, '**Assuredly, I say to you, I do not know you.'** "* (emphasis mine) The only way (let me repeat those words), THE ONLY WAY that Jesus can get to know us is when we press into the secret place in order to know Him! It's all about the oil (symbolic of the Holy Spirit). Thus the command to the rider of the black horse: "Do not harm the oil!"

One last observation: The rider had in his hand a pair of scales (a balance). This very thing represents buying and selling, merchandising, and trade. Many things effect world economics: war, famine, and weather patterns (such as drought or flooding) to name a few. When the economy is affected, the price we pay for products is effected also. The third seal (of commerce, trade, and merchandising) will be broken off the scroll and done away with. As I wrote in *The Counterfeit Woman*, the author of all trade is Satan as Ezekiel 28:15-19 says. His works come to fulfillment in the Great Babylon of the book of Revelation 18:7-19. Again, I ask you with great earnestness, please don't take or reject my word for it. Also, don't take someone else's word without studying the Word for yourself.

THE FOURTH SEAL BROKEN
A pale horse . . .
the name of him who sat on it was Death, and Hades followed.
Revelation 6:8

This fourth horse and rider is a seal that must be broken off the scroll. As Romans 5:12 and 17 says, *"Therefore, just as through*

36

one man sin entered the world, and death through sin, and thus death spread to all men, because all sinned. If by one man's offense death reigned . . ." It's obvious that death reigned from the beginning. God told Adam it would happen. It's natural that Hades would follow Death, because Hades is the place of the dead. Acts 2:27 (which is Peter quoting Psalms 16:10) says, *"You will not leave my soul in Hades, nor allow Your Holy One to see corruption."* And again Jesus speaks of Hades in the parable of the Rich man and Lazarus: *"And being in torments in Hades, he lifted up his eyes and saw Abraham afar off, and Lazarus in his bosom*." (Luke 16:23) Death and Hades are not a judgment released upon the earth when the seal is loosed or broken. Death and Hades have been around since the beginning. When it says in Revelation 6:8 "*that power was given to them over a fourth of the earth, to kill with sword, with hunger, with death, and by the beasts of the earth"*--- it is the same as Ezekiel 5:11-12 (only its the Lord speaking) *" 'Therefore, as I live,' says the Lord God, 'surely, because you have defiled My sanctuary with all your detestable things and with all your abominations, therefore I will also diminish you; My eye will not spare, nor will I have any pity. One-third of you shall die of the pestilence, and be consumed with famine in your midst; and one-third shall fall by the sword all around you; and I will scatter another third to all the winds, and I will draw out a sword after them.' "* Three-thirds equal a whole. Four one-fourths equal a whole. Power was given over a fourth of the earth to kill with sword, and a fourth of the earth to kill with hunger, and a fourth of the earth to kill with death, and a fourth of the earth to kill by the beasts of the earth. But I have very good news:
1 Corinthians 15:26 -- ***"THE LAST ENEMY THAT WILL BE DESTROYED IS DEATH."*** (emphasis mine) And then in Revelation 20:14 -- ***"DEATH AND HADES WERE CAST INTO THE LAKE OF FIRE."*** (emphasis mine)

Rejoice, Beloved!

CONSIDER THIS:

"And God **divided** the light [Day] from the darkness [Night]."
(Genesis 1:4 - emphasis mine)

"Then God said, 'Let there be lights in the firmament of the heavens to **divide** the day [light] from the night [darkness] and let them be for signs . . ." (Genesis 1:14 - emphasis mine)

"God set them in the firmament of the heavens to give light on the earth and to rule over the day [light] and over the night [darkness], and to **divide** the light [day] from the darkness [night]." (Genesis 1:17-18 - emphasis mine)

The word "divide" is mentioned three times in context of light and darkness, day and night. God is making a statement about division and separation even before man had fallen. Even before He had created man. We must take notice of this emphasis that God has made. In the gospel of John, chapter 13 and verse 30, John makes mention of Judas, saying, *"Having received the piece of bread, he then went out immediately. And it was night."* Is there more to the night then just the cycle of the sun and the absence of it?

"We love the night and in it we have created our own light!"

Our electrical grid, of which man has become accustomed, could be shut down in an instant!

In 6,000 years, we only see electricity within the last 100 where it has quickly covered the planet.

SOMETHINGS UP!

CHAPTER 4

THE FIFTH SEAL BROKEN

"I saw under the altar the souls of those who had been slain for the word of God and for the testimony that they held."
Revelation 6:9

I began to write this chapter on the fifth seal, but the Lord wouldn't let me continue. After a few days, He began to show me His heart over the content of this seal. This is very dear to His heart and I found myself in fear and trembling as I prepared to write about this seal. The Psalmist in Psalms 116:15 has a revelation of God's heart on this matter: *"Precious in the sight of the Lord is the death of His saints."* He takes their death very seriously, because death is not a part of His kingdom; neither are the ones who kill His precious people. There is only One worthy of breaking this seal! He is the *Lamb* that was also slain. Jesus experienced the very thing that these souls under the altar experienced. Their hearts are most intricately bonded together. As we begin to uncover hidden mysteries in this seal, we will see the very heart of God on these things. There is a story that unfolds in the gospel of Matthew from chapter 21 through chapter 24:1. It begins with Jesus coming to Jerusalem for the last time. He comes in riding on a donkey colt and the multitudes were praising Him as king. It says the whole city was moved. The first thing that Jesus does when He arrives is to go into the temple and drive out the merchandisers, overturn tables and chairs, and proclaim that they (the religious rulers) had made it a den of thieves. This is not your typical "politically correct" way for a king to make His entrance. After this happened, the blind and lame came to Him in the temple and He healed them. Jesus had just turned the temple from a den of thieves back into a house of prayer and healing broke out. He then left the temple to lodge in Bethany that night. On His way back to the temple the very next day, He cursed a fig tree and it died immediately. He told His disciples that if they had faith, they could do the same. He also said to them, *"But also if you say to this mountain, 'Be removed and be cast into the sea,' it will be done."* (Matthew 21:21) Jesus was just about to face a mountain with the religious leaders. He came back into the temple and the chief priests and elders confronted Him immediately concerning His outrages acts in the temple the previous day.

JESUS SPEAKS TO A MOUNTAIN

Within the next several verses, we see Jesus in turn confronting them through parables. You can read these parables, but I will only point out a verse from each one that expresses the heart of God towards these religious leaders:

The parable of the two sons (prodigal son): *"Assuredly, I say to you that tax collectors and harlots enter the kingdom of God before you."* (Matthew 21:31)

The parable of the wicked vinedressers: *"Therefore I say to you, the kingdom of God will be taken from you and given to a nation bearing the fruits of it."* (Matthew 21:43)

42

The parable of the wedding feast: *"When the king heard about it, he was furious. And he sent out his armies, destroyed those murderers, and burned up their city."* (Matthew 22:7)

This very thing spoken of in Matthew 22:7 happened 40 years later when Rome destroyed Jerusalem and burnt the temple as Jesus had also predicted in Matthew 24:2. In Matthew 23:2-3, Jesus does give a little respect to the scribes and Pharisees by telling His followers to observe what they say, because they sit in Moses' seat; but do not do as they do. Jesus then begins addressing this mountain. He pronounces eight "woes" against the scribes and Pharisees. Within each one of these "woes," He is pointing out the hypocrisy of the scribes and Pharisees. It's the last "woe" that sets the stage for the fifth seal. *"Woe to you, scribes and Pharisees, hypocrites! Because you build the tombs of the prophets and adorn the monuments of the righteous, and say, 'If we had lived in the days of our fathers, we would not have been partakers with them in the blood of the prophets.' Therefore you are witnesses against yourselves that you are sons of those who murdered the prophets. Fill up, then, the measure of your fathers guilt. Serpents, brood of vipers! How can you escape the condemnation of hell? Therefore, indeed, I send you prophets, wise men, and scribes: some of them you will kill and crucify, and some of them you will scourge in your synagogues and persecute from city to city, **that on you may come all the righteous blood shed on the earth, from the blood of righteous Abel to the blood of Zechariah, son of Berechiah, whom you murdered between the temple and the altar.***" (emphasis mine) Needless to say, the scribes and Pharisees of that day had not lived in the day of Abel or Zechariah. Yet all the blood of these righteous men was on them! They were the rulers of that day twisting and perverting the way of the Lord and persecuting and killing those who walked in the way of righteousness. We can see this very thing in the harlot of Revelation 17 and 18. *"I saw the woman, drunk with the blood of the saints and with the blood of the martyrs of Jesus"* (Revelation 17:6). *"And in her was found the blood of prophets and saints, and of all who were slain on the earth"* (Revelation 18:24). Then in Revelation 19:2, we see the judgment of the harlot because of these things: *"True and righteous are His judgments, because He* *has judged the great harlot who corrupted the earth with her fornication;* **and He has avenged on her the blood of His servants shed by her."** (emphasis mine) Just as the scribes and Pharisees had the blood of all the righteous from Abel to Zechariah on them because they persecuted and killed those that where sent to them, so the harlot also has the blood of all the righteous on her. We must take very seriously the words in Revelation 18:4-6 that addresses us as believers: *"Come out of her, my people, lest you share in her sins, and lest you receive of her plagues. For her sins have reached to heaven, and God has remembered her iniquities. (Repay to her what she herself has paid [to others]and double [her doom] in accordance with what she has done. Mix a double portion for her in the cup she mixed [for others]).* (AMP) The very hypocrisy that the harlot and the religious leaders lived in was the point of judgment that came to them. We must walk far from hypocrisy and walk humbly with God before His people. I can think of two examples at this very time on earth that could get a believer slain for the word of God. The first one would be in regard to the homosexual agenda. If a believer would take what the word of God says on this subject and preach it in love without compromise, that believer could eventually face possible death because of the militancy of the gay agenda. Conviction of the Holy Spirit would be released and people would come to Jesus and be delivered from that lifestyle. How do you think that would effect those who are militantly proclaiming that they were born that way? The other example would be in regard to Islam and what they believe. They believe that Allah is God and that Mohammed is their prophet. If a believer would preach Jesus, in love, as the **only** way, truth, and life; how would this threaten the Muslim who only adheres to what the Koran proclaims? I challenge you to try this in a Muslim neighborhood. Today, if you convert to Christianity from Islam, you have committed an offence worthy of death! You don't even have to preach Jesus; you just profess that you are now a Christian. If you are aware of what is going on in the middle eastern nations, you will know that those who believe in Jesus are being put to death at an alarming rate.

THE DEAD CRYING OUT

You will notice those under the altar are crying out with a loud voice, saying, *"How long, O Lord, holy and true, until You judge and avenge our blood on those who dwell on the earth?"* Who were these people under the altar? (I'm sure the historian Josephus could add many to this list.) I see the very first one was Abel, after him Ahimelech (the priest Saul had killed), Abner (whom Joab had murdered), Jezebel massacred many Prophets; she will have much blood on her hands. The list goes on through the Prophets and into the New Testament: Stephen, Peter, James, and as Hebrews proclaims; *"Others were tortured, not accepting deliverance, that they might obtain a better resurrection."* (Hebrews 11:35) And again: *"They were stoned, they were sawn in two, they were slain with the sword."* (Hebrews 11:37) Beloved, we are seeing Christians being slaughtered at this very moment. Multitudes without number are under the altar. Abel is still crying out in prayer, "How long till You judge and avenge our blood?" This is the unified cry coming from all of these that have been slain. They were told to rest a little while longer until the number was completed. There was a number (known by God), of those who would be killed for the word of God and the testimony that they walked in. This number would be reached and then He would avenge their blood. How close are we to reaching that number? Many Muslim nations in this present day are killing Christians and driving them from their land. ISIS has risen up and has killed many Christians and burned down their homes and churches. This seal, which has never been addressed since Abel's murder has to be broken off and addressed before the scroll can be read. The *Lamb* that was slain, just as the souls under the altar were, was slain outside the camp (Hebrews 13:12). His blood was then brought into the Holy Place (verse 11) and the veil of the temple was torn in two from top to bottom (Matthew 27:51). God just opened the door to His presence for all to come in. Being Jew or Gentile, God does not take the murdering of His saints lightly. Many would ask, "Where is the justice for the murdered saints?" The Lord has never missed seeing a martyr's blood being spilled. This seal is not a judgment loosed, but the awaiting of a number to be fulfilled so justice can prevail; then judgment will be loosed. Their blood will be avenged when the last martyr is killed for the word of God and for the testimony that he holds. In the parable of the wheat and tares, the owner of the field answers the servants that asked him about gathering up the tares: *". . . No* (don't gather them), *lest while you gather up the tares you also uproot the wheat with them. Let them grow together until the harvest, and at the time of the harvest I will say to the reapers, 'First gather together the tares and bind them in bundles to burn them, but gather the wheat into my barn.' "* (Matthew 13:24-30) Jesus is giving a glimpse into the Father's heart as to why there seems to be such a delay in avenging their blood. *"He is patient and is not willing for anyone to perish, but for all to come to repentance."* (II Peter 3:9) Paul killed Christians, yet he was wonderfully saved. If the Lord would have avenged their blood during Paul's time, Paul would not be in the Lord's presence today.

THE ALTAR

If we read in Exodus 29, we will see the Lord giving Moses instruction on the consecration of Aaron and his sons for the priesthood. These instructions were given to Moses while he was on the mountain for 40 days and nights meeting with God. In verse 10, it says they were to bring a bull and lay hands on the bull's head and then kill the bull before the Lord. They were then to take some of the blood and put it on the horns of the altar and pour out the rest at the base of the altar. In verses 36-37 of chapter 29 it says, *"And you shall offer a bull every day as a sin offering for atonement. You shall cleanse the altar when you make atonement for it, and you shall anoint it to sanctify it. Seven days you shall make atonement for the altar and sanctify it. And the altar shall be most holy. Whatever touches the altar must be holy."* We see in these passages that blood was poured out and the altar was to be most holy before the Lord. Nothing unclean or full of darkness could touch the altar. John was seeing souls under the altar.

We also see in Leviticus chapters 4 and 5 that the blood of the sin offering and the trespass offering was to be poured out at the base of the altar. When a person, anointed priest or of the whole congregation of Israel, sins unintentionally, the blood of their sacrifice was also taken and applied to the horns of the altar of incense. (Leviticus 4:7 and 18) So we have the altar of burnt offering

46

and the altar of incense made holy by the blood of the sacrifice. The golden altar of incense was consecrated and made holy with the holy anointing oil (Exodus 30:26-27) which was talked about under the third seal. You will notice that the "golden altar" is also mentioned in Revelation 8:3 and 9:13. Are they all connected? The angel in chapter 8 came and stood at the altar. The altar the souls were under? Were the prayers of those under the altar also offered with the incense that the angel burned on the golden altar which was before God? Could it be that judgment started when the angel in Chapter 8 filled his golden censer with fire from the altar and threw it to the earth? In chapter 9:13 when a voice was heard from the four horns of the golden altar saying, *"Release the four angels who are bound at the great river Euphrates,"* could it be that the Lord was avenging the blood of those under the altar at this time?

We know the scribes and Pharisees and the religious leaders of that day have innocent blood on their hands. The harlot of Revelation also has innocent blood on her hands. Jesus perceived it correctly: It's the hypocrisy of the religious that kills those who stand for the word of God and carry a testimony that they are of God. It's the hypocrisy of the religious that kills prophets, saints, and all those who were slain on the earth. Some would say right here, "It's the ungodly that kill Christians! It's ISIS (Islamic state of Iraq and Syria) that are killing Christians!" I would have to answer with this: Talk to any Muslim extremist about Christians and how they live their lives in this day and age, and they will tell you of their hypocrisy. They see that most people who call themselves a Christian or follower of Jesus live a lifestyle that does not glorify God. They see hypocrisy. They see one who names His name, but lives so full of the world. Yes, they serve a god who is violent and destructive and is very rigid toward outward holiness, but there are very few today that make Christianity desirable. We, as the Gentile Church, are to make Israel jealous so they will turn to their Messiah. Instead, many in the Church have become a stench to the rest of the world, because they refuse to radically abandon themselves to the God who bought them. I know this is a harsh word. We must wake up! We must press into God in the secret place that He may reward us openly. It's His glory upon our lives that changes the world. Our compromise with the world brings a stench to the world. If the world sees itself in the Christian, then God is no different than they are. If the world sees Jesus in the Christian, then God will draw men to Himself. We all must continually come into the secret place with God daily (moment by moment) because we all leak. I am not satisfied with being baptized in the Holy Spirit just one time. I need baptized over and over and over again!

The fifth seal is the waiting, unaddressed, spilled blood of the martyrs crying out from under the altar. Only Jesus, the *Lamb* that was also slain, can break off this seal!

CHAPTER 5

DICTATORS MUST BE BROKEN

BREAKING THE SIXTH SEAL

"The stars of heaven fell . . . the sky receded as a scroll . . . and the kings of the earth, the great men, the rich men, the commanders, the mighty men, every slave and every free man hid themselves . . . from the face of Him who sits on the throne and from the wrath of the Lamb!" Revelation 6:12-17

There is a great shaking coming; not just to earth, but also to the heavens. Haggai 2:6-7 says it this way, *"For thus says the Lord of hosts: 'Once more, in a little while, I will shake the heavens and earth, the sea and dry land; and I will shake all nations, and they shall come to the Desire of All Nations.' "* The writer of Hebrews also points this out: *"Now He has given a promise: Yet once more I will shake and make tremble not only the earth but also the [starry] heavens. "* (Hebrews 12:26 - AMP) Man who considers himself great, mighty, rich, and in charge does not consider God's ways nor does he even tremble when he hears His word. You will notice who is specifically addressed in this seal: kings, great men, mighty men, etc. They are all in charge of the earth; so they think! The earth has ever increasingly been ruled by the ungodly since Cain. Cain did not respect God in his offering to Him. In turn, God did not respect Cain's offering. Cain became very angry and killed his brother Abel, whose offering was accepted. God's punishment on Cain did not bring him to repent and Cain's response, which is recorded in Genesis 4:16, was to turn his back on God and leave His presence. Seeing what happens next is important. Genesis 4:17 says that Cain knew his wife and a whole generation of wickedness was started. He built a city and named it after his first son. His great, great, great grandson Lamech, passed on Cain's wickedness and rejection of God. Lamech's sons also lived outside of the presence of God, but were pointed out in Scripture as great men. Notice the emphasis on their accomplishments: *"Jabel was the father of those who dwell in tents and have livestock . . . Jubal was the father of all those who play the harp and flute* (music) *. . . Tubal-cain was the instructor of every craftsman."* (Genesis 4:20-22) All these dealt with the trading of merchandise. Genesis 6 says that man began to multiply on the earth and those from the lineage of Seth (sons in God's likeness, see Genesis 5:1-3) began to marry whoever they wanted from those who went out of God's presence. The result, giants like Goliath, is recorded in Genesis 6:4-5: *"These were the **mighty men** who were of old, men of renown. Then the Lord saw that the wickedness of man was great in the earth, and that every intent of the thoughts of his heart was only evil continually."* (emphasis mine) God's response to what He had just seen: The Flood! After the flood we see Noah's relatives becoming **great** and **mighty men** of the earth. The grandsons of Noah (Genesis 10:2) Javan, Tubal, and Meshech were mentioned in Ezekiel 27:13 as traders. They bartered human lives . . . for the luxury merchandise in the city of Tyre, Raamah, Sheba, and Dedan. Grandsons of Ham (who saw Noah's nakedness) were also mentioned in Ezekiel 27:15, 20,22-23. They were also great traders. In Revelation 18:23, we see that the merchants (traders) who are in Great Babylon were the **great men** of the earth. Merchants were **great men** in Tyre's day and merchants are considered **great men** in this present age. Now to mention another one of Noah's relatives who went on to be a mighty man. *"Nimrod who began to be a* **mighty** *one on the earth. He was a* **mighty** *hunter before the Lord; therefore it is said, 'Like Nimrod the* **mighty** *hunter before the Lord.' And the beginning of his kingdom was Babel . . . in the land of Shinar. From that land he went on to Assyria and built Nineveh."* (Genesis 10:8-11 - emphasis mine) The results of Nimrod's mightiness brought forth Babylon. You can read the Prophets to see what became of this city. The conception of this city, Babel, can be found in Genesis 11:1-9, which resulted with God saying, *"Behold, they are one people and they have all one language; and this is only the beginning of what they will do, and now nothing they have imagined they can do will be impossible for them."* They were becoming great and mighty in their own eyes. What does this say about us in this present day? Have we come to the place where nothing that we have imagined we can do will be impossible for us? The prophet Jonah went to Nineveh and prophesied against it because of its wickedness. Yes, they repented in 800 B.C. at the preaching of Jonah, but later in 647 B.C., judgment is spoken against her. In this present day, Nineveh is in Iraq. We can see from just these few Scriptures how man's greatness and mightiness has led him to the place we observe in the book of Revelation under the fifth seal: *"Hide us* (mountains and rocks) *from the face of Him who sits on the throne and from the wrath of the Lamb!"* This very statement *"The wrath of the Lamb"* says that Jesus is also storing up wrath against His enemies. It's a strong possibility that because of the souls under the altar, who's blood was shed for the word of God and for the testimony that they held, that Jesus Himself is full of wrath. I know to some of you it seems impossible that Jesus could be full of wrath. Yet the Scripture is clear: They were wanting to be hidden from the wrath of the *Lamb.* We must remember that God's wrath is not like our wrath. Our wrath is more like rage and not motivated by love. We must trust that the Lord is perfect in all His ways; even when He is full of wrath.

THE SHAKING OF THE HEAVENS

"The sun became black as sackcloth of hair, and the moon became like blood. And the stars of heaven fell to the earth, as a fig tree drops its late figs when it is shaken by a mighty wind. Then the

52

sky receded as a scroll when it is rolled up" (Revelation 6:12-14). To understand what is happening when we start to see these things, we must go to Genesis 1:14, where God is creating the earth and the heavens: *"Then God said, 'Let there be lights in the firmament of the heavens to divide the day from the night; and **let them be for signs.'** "* (emphasis mine) Here we see that God created the sun, moon, and stars not just to inhabit the heavens for light by day and night; nor did He create stars just for star gazing. He created them for a sign. Did God need to create signs for Himself in order to know when certain events would take place? No! These were to be signs for us to know when events would take place. There are many Scriptures that speak of the sun, moon, and stars indicating when certain things or events would take place. Jesus knew what it said in Genesis 1:14; He also knew what these Scriptures were indicating.

Isaiah 13:9-10 --- *"Behold, the day of the Lord comes, cruel, with both wrath and fierce anger, to lay the land desolate; and He will destroy its sinners from it. For the stars of heaven and their constellations will not give their light; the sun will be darkened in its going forth, and the moon will not cause its light to shine."*

Joel 2:30-31 --- *"And I will show wonders in the heavens and in the earth: Blood and fire and pillars of smoke. The sun shall be turned to darkness, and the moon into blood, before the coming of the great and awesome day of the Lord."*

Joel 3:14-16 --- *"Multitudes, multitudes in the valley of decision! For the day of the Lord is near in the valley of decision. The sun and moon will grow dark, and the stars will diminish their brightness. The Lord also will roar from Zion, and utter His voice from Jerusalem; the heavens and earth will shake; but the Lord will be a shelter for His people!"*

Amos 8:9 --- *"And it shall come to pass in that day,"* says the Lord God, *"That I will make the sun go down at noon, and I will darken the earth in broad daylight."*

Luke 21:25-27 --- *"And there will be signs in the sun, in the moon, and in the stars . . . for the powers of the heavens will be shaken. Then they will see the Son of Man coming in a cloud with power and great glory."* Jesus seems to be making a direct referral to Genesis 1:14 concerning signs.

Revelation 6:13 (AMP) --- *" . . . the stars of the sky dropped to the earth like a fig tree shedding its unripe fruit out of season when shaken by a strong wind."* This is not a new proclamation from the Lord. The Lord proclaims this very thing through the Prophet Isaiah in chapter 34:4 (AMP) *"All the host of the heavens shall be dissolved and crumble away, and the skies shall be rolled together like a scroll; and all their host [the stars and the planets] shall drop like a faded leaf from a vine, and like a withered fig from a fig tree."* The Lord through Isaiah is confirming the very thing that He is also saying in the book of Revelation in regard to the stars falling like a fig from a fig tree. They are shaken free and fall to the earth in large groups when strong winds blow against them. Since figs are related to stars in these Scriptures, we can conclude that the stars will be falling because of something much greater than themselves. When Scripture mentions stars falling, it is a sign of something else falling.

THE CASTING OF SATAN OUT OF HEAVEN

In Revelation 9:1, we see a star fallen from heaven to earth: ***"I saw a star that had fallen from the sky to the earth***; *and to the* **angel** *was given the key of the shaft of the abyss (the bottomless pit)."* (AMP - emphasis mine) This Scripture plainly states that the star was an angel; a fallen angel. In Isaiah 14:12 it says, *"How you are* **fallen from heaven**, *O Lucifer, son of the morning! How you are* **cut down to the ground**." (emphasis mine) Ezekiel 28:12-17 also says, *"You were the seal of perfection . . . you were in Eden . . . you were the anointed cherub who covers . . . you were on the holy mountain of God . . . you were perfect in your ways from the day you* *were created, till iniquity was found in you. By the abundance of your trading you became filled with violence within, and you sinned; therefore **I cast you as a profane thing out of the mountain of God**. Your heart was lifted up . . . you corrupted your wisdom . . . **I cast you to the ground**."* (emphasis mine) In both of these references it is plainly Satan that is being talked about. Jesus had sent 70 of His followers out to evangelize. They returned saying that even the demons were subject to them in His name. Jesus' response is most interesting. He indicates what He was seeing in the Spirit as they were taking authority over demons: *"I saw Satan **falling like a lightning [flash] from heaven**."* (AMP - emphasis mine) Again, we see Satan falling from heaven, but has he fallen to earth yet? Revelation 12 expounds on two signs from heaven that John had seen. We will look at the second sign that addresses the Dragon (Satan). You can read this on your own, but I would like to start at verse 7. *"War broke out in heaven; Michael and his angels fought with the dragon."* I must stop here and point out the fact that this Scripture indicates that Satan is still in heaven at this time! Continuing. *"Michael and his angels fought with the dragon; and the dragon and his angels fought, but they did not prevail, nor was a place found for them in heaven any longer. So the great dragon was cast out, that serpent of old, called the Devil and Satan, who deceives the whole world; he was cast to the earth, and his angels were cast out with him."* Remember this is the Revelation of Jesus Christ, which God gave Him to show His servants---*things which must shortly take place.* Satan being cast out of heaven to earth has not happened yet! He being cast out is a sign of the last days. It happens in the time period of the two witnesses in Jerusalem and the woman (true Israel) being saved and divinely protected for three and one half years. Continuing in verse 10: *"Then I heard a loud voice saying in heaven, 'Now salvation, and strength, and the kingdom of our God, and the power of His Christ have come, for the accuser of our brethren, who accused them before our God day and night, has been cast down.'"* John heard this multitude of people speaking from heaven and addressing their brethren. Those speaking from heaven continue: *"And they overcame him* (Satan) *by the blood of the Lamb and by the word of their testimony, and they did not love their lives to the death. Therefore rejoice, O heavens, and you who dwell in them! Woe to the inhabitants of the earth and the sea! For* *the devil has come down to you, having great wrath, because he knows that he has a short time."* The very thing that was prophesied in Isaiah 14 and Ezekiel 28 in regard to Satan being cast out of heaven and cast to the ground is fulfilled in these verses of Scripture. I believe these brethren that are talked about are Jews who have believed and they, through their overcoming, have caused Satan to be cast out of heaven. It says he was cast to the earth and because this happened they are saying, "Woe to the earth." Yet he has also been cast out of heaven for which they express, *"Therefore rejoice, O heavens, and you who dwell in them!"* Paul talks of dwelling in the heavens in his letter to the Colossians, *"Set your mind on things above, not on things on the earth. For you died, and your life is hidden with Christ in God. When Christ who is our life appears, then you also will appear with Him in glory."* (Colossians 3:2-4) I can only imagine what it will be like with Satan gone from the heavenlies. No temptations! No warfare! No wicked thoughts! Only the presence of God with those who dwell in the heavens! When I pray, I will only experience God's presence. There will be no temptation intercepting our conversations with our Father. No lustful thoughts when we are listening to the message on Sunday morning. Satan is not in the heavenlies anymore. If you think this is too simplistic, please, I challenge you to study for yourself.

God is using His people to fulfill His plans and purposes to eradicate all evil and wickedness. It looks bad for the earth, but the enemy is being put under His feet! This is what the writer of Hebrews 2:6-8 is indicating concerning man when it says, *"What is man that You are mindful of him, or the son of man that You take care of him? You have made him a little lower than the angels; You have crowned him with glory and honor, and set him over the works of Your hands. **You have put all things under his feet.** For in that He put **all** in subjection under him, He **left nothing** that is not put under him."* (emphasis mine) The fact that Satan is cast to the earth and "woe" is pronounced to the inhabitants of the earth means that something very evil has come to the earth.

MOUNTAINS AND ROCKS

"And the kings of the earth, the great men, the rich men, the commanders, the mighty men, every slave and every free man, hid themselves in the caves and in the rocks of the mountains."
Revelation 6:15

For many years, when I would read this verse, I would envision all these people literally running and hiding in the mountains. I would ask myself a dumb question, "Well what if there were no mountains where these people lived, where would they hide?" As I studied the word, I began to see that the mountains that were talked about are not actual mountains, but belief systems that people surround themselves with. As I mentioned in the fifth seal, Jesus addressed a mountain at the same time that He cursed a fig tree. The mountain was the religious, godless men of that day and their belief system concerning who God was and how to walk according to the law of Moses. This belief system had blinded their eyes from seeing Jesus as their Messiah. They had become the great and mighty men in Israel.

I'm not out to try and convince you of these things. You must study them on your own. There are numerous Scriptures that address mountains. As you study these you will begin to see that when the word mountain appears, it means much more than a literal pile of rocks.

Just a note on the word "rocks": David's rock can be found in Psalm 61:2 and 62:2,6,7: *"Lead me to the rock that is higher than I." "He only is my rock and my salvation." "The rock of my strength, and my refuge, is in God."*

Peter's rock can be found in Matthew 16:16. *"You are the Christ, the Son of the living God."*

These men under the sixth seal are running and hiding into their belief systems (the caves and the rocks of the mountains). It's the same as when *"Adam and his wife hid themselves from the presence of the Lord among the trees of the garden."* (Genesis 3:8)

THERE'S JUST SOMETHING ABOUT THAT FACE!
"Fall on us and hide us from the face of Him who sits on the throne."
Revelation 6:16

There's just something about that face! What is it that causes so much fear in these men that would cause kings to run and hide? What is it in His face that would cause commanders and wealthy men to run and hide? They do not want to see His face! When you look into another person's face, they will usually display one of two things: Acceptance or rejection depending on what you have done to them. Both of these responses have strong feelings and actions connected with them. Will there be something very terrible in the face of love when it has been rejected and trampled on? As you will see in the verse below, Moses, *". . . who was very humble, more than all men on the earth"* (Numbers12:3), he was not able to see God's face.

Exodus 33:20 --- *"You cannot see My face; for no man shall see Me, and live."* If Moses, a very humble man, could not see His face, then what will happen to sinners and the rebellious when they do? Peter brings out in his letter that judgment begins with the house of God. Then he says, *"If it begins with us first, what will be the end of those **who do not obey the gospel** of God?"* (1Peter 4:17 - emphasis mine) The fact that kings, great men, rich men, and commanders were mentioned seems to indicate they were the decision makers of the earth. The ones who rule and enforce their will and mandates on every one else. Yet the phrase *"every slave and every free man"* indicates that this seal involves all men everywhere. Those mentioned as slaves and free did not want to see His face either. We must remember the seven seals are to be broken off of the scroll. The sixth seal, as well as the fifth seal, seem to indicate past, present, and future situations and people as pointed out above. It sounds like the earth is full of wickedness and when the great day of His wrath has come, all those will be called into account. One more question for those who only see Jesus as a loving *Lamb* and not a judge: When it says in Revelation 6:17 *"the great day of **His wrath** has come"* (emphasis mine), who is being mentioned concerning "His wrath": God or Jesus? Yes, Jesus loves us, but there will come a day when all men will stand before Him, face to face, and they will either hear the words "Well done faithful one" or "I don't know you or where you are from"!

CONSIDER THIS:

We have seen in the last chapter *"The great day of His wrath has come, and who is able to stand?"* In Revelation 7:1-3, we immediately see four angels who are ready to bring destruction upon the earth. We also see that it was **granted** to them to harm the earth and the sea. As it was also **granted or given** to the riders in the first, second, and fourth seal. (This must be carefully discerned so that there will be no deception.) We can see from other sources of Scripture that God was the one who granted these things. One of these Scriptures is in Exodus 12:23: *"For the Lord will pass through to strike the Egyptians; and when He sees the blood on the lintel and on the two doorposts, the Lord will pass over the door and **not allow the destroyer*** (not grant the destroyer power) *to come into your houses to strike you."* (emphasis mine) This only affected the Egyptians. It effected those who did not apply the blood on their doorposts. What kept the destroyer from being granted the power to destroy was that the Lord observed the obedience of His people in what He had told them to do. Another example is in Job 1:12 and 2:6, *"And the Lord said to Satan, 'Behold, all that he* (Job) *has is in your power; only do not lay a hand on his person.' "* And again, *"And the Lord said to Satan, 'Behold, he is in your hand, but spare his life.' "* Again, the Lord granted these things and it was Job's obedience that kept him from being destroyed. I'm not sure why these things were granted, but they were granted with a command from God Himself as was the case in the third seal, *"Do not harm the oil and the wine."* God commanded Satan not to harm or take Job's life!

In the granting of destruction to the four angels, God had given a command through another angel directly to these four angels saying, *"Do not harm the earth, the sea, or the trees **till** we have sealed the servants of our God on their foreheads."* (Revelation 9:4 - emphasis mine) In other words, there was to be no wrath or destruction released over the entire earth until all 144,000 Israeli servants were sealed. Again, this very command is evidence that the first four seals are not judgments released upon the earth, but they are seals of past and prevailing judgments keeping the scroll from being opened and fulfilled in its entirety.

As the 144,000 are Jews, mentioned in Revelation 7:3-8, so the multitudes without number, as described in Revelation 7:9-17, are Gentiles. Could this possibly be what Paul describes in Romans 11:25-26 regarding both Jew and Gentile? *"For I do not desire, brethren, that you should be ignorant of this mystery, lest you should be wise in your own opinion, that blindness in part has happened to Israel **until the fullness of the Gentiles** has come in. And so **all Israel will be saved.**"* (emphasis mine) Is what we see described in chapter 7 the mystery of the fullness of the Gentiles coming in and the Jews being saved? These things would also be within the context of the sixth seal which also must be broken off the scroll in order for it to be read.

CHAPTER 6

SILENCE

". . . there was silence in heaven . . ."
Revelation 8:1

THE SEVENTH SEAL BROKEN

Why was there silence? Up to this point, there had been lightnings and thunderings and voices coming from the throne! There has been weeping and singing and loud proclamations! Voices like thunder! Loud voices crying out from under the altar! Great men crying out "Hide us!" Angels crying out with a loud voices, "Do not harm the earth, sea, or trees until God's Jewish servants are sealed!" Great multitudes crying out with a loud voice, "Salvation belongs to our God who sits on the throne, and to the

Lamb!" Then silence! Something was up! Zephaniah proclaims: *"Be silent in the presence of the Lord God; for the day of the Lord is at hand."* (Zephaniah 1:7) Something was about to happen that would change everything.

I believe the last three seals are all tied together:

- Fifth seal ---Slain souls under the altar crying out.
- Sixth seal --- Rulers and all men great, rich, mighty, etc. in fear of seeing judgment coming.
- Seventh seal --- Seven angels proclaiming and releasing judgment through an angel standing at the altar throwing fire to the earth.

The souls under the altar had been murdered. Each one of them was killed by someone who was either a ruler giving the order to do so, by someone who hated what they stood for, or by someone who was doing it in service to his god. All of those under the sixth seal cannot be put in this category; but we must remember the words of Jesus in Matthew 23:35, where Jesus was addressing the scribes and Pharisees because of their resistance to believing in Him. Jesus proclaimed eight woes against them and then told them, *"On you may come all the righteous blood shed on the earth, from the blood of righteous Abel to the blood of Zechariah, whom you murdered between the temple and the altar."* These men had nothing to do directly with Abel's murder! Yet Abel's blood was on their heads! Jesus just blamed the scribes and Pharisees for his death. To the natural mind this doesn't make sense, but in Jesus' mind they represented the very ones throughout history that were to blame for the death of the martyrs. We must take notice of what Jesus said of them. He said they were like white-washed tombs. They outwardly appeared righteous, but inside they were full of hypocrisy and lawlessness. Since lawlessness will be on the increase in the last days and the love of many will grow cold, we must guard our hearts against this. I have met people who say they are believers and look good on the outside, yet walk in lawlessness and hypocrisy. Their love (for God and man) had grown cold because of their ongoing resistance to His voice. This leads us into the seventh seal:

"When He opened the seventh seal, there was silence in heaven for about half and hour. And I saw the seven angels who stand before God, and to them were given seven trumpets." (Revelation 8:1-2)

We will see in the next few verses that trumpets are for proclaiming some kind of disaster coming very quickly. They are not bringing the disaster, they are warning of a coming disaster.

Ezekiel 33:1-5 --- *Again the word of the Lord came to me, saying, "Son of man, speak to the children of your people, and say to them: 'When I bring the sword upon a land, and the people of the land take a man from their territory and make him their watchman, when he sees the sword coming upon the land, if he blows the **trumpet** and warns the people, then whoever hears the sound of the **trumpet** and does not take warning, if the sword comes and takes him away, his blood shall be on his own head. He heard the sound of the **trumpet**, but did not take warning; his blood shall be upon himself. But he who takes warning will save his life.'"* (emphasis mine)

Jeremiah 4:19 -- *"O my soul, my soul! I am pained in my very heart! My heart makes a noise in me; I cannot hold my peace, because you have heard, O my soul, the sound of the **trumpet**, the alarm of war."* (emphasis mine) Jeremiah had been warning Israel that Babylon was coming because they refused to turn back to God, even though many prophets had been sent to them and entreated them to repent. The Lord was actually reminding Jeremiah of what Moses had spoken to Israel in Deuteronomy 28:49-50 if they didn't listen to the Lord or observe His commands. *"The Lord will bring a nation against you from afar, from the end of the earth, as swift as the eagle flies . . . a nation of fierce countenance, which does not respect the elderly nor show favor to the young."* Jeremiah was blowing a trumpet, calling Israel to repent!

Zephaniah 1:14-15 -- *"The great day of the Lord is near .
. . That day is a day of wrath, a day of trouble and distress,
a day of devastation and desolation, a day of darkness and
gloominess, a day of clouds and thick darkness, a day of
trumpet and alarm!"* (emphasis mine)

Joel 2:1 -- *"Blow the **trumpet** in Zion, and sound an
alarm in My holy mountain! Let all the inhabitants of the
land tremble; For the day of the Lord is coming!"* (emphasis
mine)

The seven angels in Revelation were given seven trumpets in
order to warn the inhabitants of the earth that something was
coming. Something of great magnitude. As we continue in
Revelation 8:3-6, we will see why the trumpets are going to be
blown.

*"Then another angel, having a golden censer, came and
stood at the altar. He was given much incense, that he
should offer it with the prayers of all the saints upon the
golden altar which was before the throne. And the smoke of
the incense, with the prayers of the saints, ascended before
God from the angel's hand. Then the angel took the censer,
filled it with fire from the altar, and threw it to the earth.
And there were noises, thunderings, lightnings, and an
earthquake. So the seven angels who had the seven
trumpets prepared themselves to sound."*

Up to this point there had been silence as the angel offered
the incense with the saint's prayers. You will notice that the angel is
standing at the altar. The very altar that the slain souls were under.
The angel offered their prayers along with all the saint's prayers
upon the golden altar which was before the throne. Yes, there is a
golden altar before the throne in heaven! Some believers think all
which was in the tabernacle was done away with when Christ came.
Remember, Moses was to make all things according to what was in
heaven already. These souls that are crying out under the altar are
seeing their prayers fulfilled. The angel then takes fire from the altar
(that the slain souls were under) and throws it to the earth. The

silence has ended as described in Revelation 8:5 (AMP): *"Then there followed peals of thunder and loud rumblings and blasts and noises, and flashes of lightning and an earthquake."* To all movie goers, this is not Hollywood expressing itself on the golden screen. This is the Lord expressing Himself because of all that has piled up high before His throne! There has been a storehouse of wickedness, so to speak. It has been stored up to this point and now all things must be accomplished according to His plan. What was described in Zechariah's vision (Zechariah 5:1-4) concerning the flying scroll and written on it the words: *"This is the curse that goes out over the face of the whole earth: Every thief shall be expelled, according to this side of the scroll; and , every perjurer shall be expelled, according to that side of it."* This and the woman in the basket represent all the wicked of the earth. Also in his vision the woman in the basket has had a house built for it and has been set on that base as described in Zechariah 5:5-11. The house being built will be set in the land of Shinar, which is in the region of Babylon (present day Iraq). At this time in history, we will see the words of Jesus fulfilled as mentioned in Matthew 24:21, *"For then there will be great tribulation, such as has not been since the beginning of the world until this time, no, nor ever shall be."* Amplified brings it even more clear: *"For then there will be great tribulation (affliction, distress, and oppression) such as has not been from the beginning of the world until now--no, **and never will be [again]."*** (emphasis mine) Don't you just long for that day when all this garbage will be done away with! Praise God He has the last word!

SOUNDING SEVEN TRUMPETS

What I am about to write is what I have received from the Lord. Don't take (or reject) what I am about to say until you have studied it for yourself. Remember Revelation 1:1, *"The Revelation of Jesus Christ, which God gave Him **to show His servants**--things which must shortly take place."* (emphasis mine) As we look into the trumpet judgments we must realize that these seven judgments are why the seventh seal needed to be broken off the scroll. These judgments are within the confines of the seventh and last seal. It must be broken off in order to read the scroll.

I believe the first four trumpet judgments are only warnings given and not judgments released at that time. They are fulfilled in and along with the sixth trumpet judgment. This is the evidence of why I believe this:

1) Back in Revelation 7:1-3, there are four angels ready to harm the earth and the sea. They have been commanded by an angel who is putting a seal on Jewish servants not to do any harm or release judgment upon the earth and sea until these Jewish servants are sealed. They have been stopped or bound. Then in Revelation 8:7-13 which explains the first four trumpet judgments, we see that they effect the earth and sea. They are four angels blowing trumpets of warning as Revelation 8:6 says, ***"They prepared themselves** to sound."* (emphasis mine) They only prepared themselves; they were not releasing judgment. Then we jump ahead and see the sixth angel sounding the trumpet, and a voice from the four horns of the golden altar saying, *"Release the four angels who are bound at the great river Euphrates. So the four angels, **who had been prepared**. . . were released to kill <u>a third</u> of mankind"* (Revelation 9:14-15 - emphasis mine) (Again, please study this for yourself.)

2) We see in the first trumpet judgment that <u>a third</u> of the earth was burned up, along with <u>a third</u> of the trees, and **all** green grass. If this judgment was carried out at that time, then there would be no grass because it was all burned up. We see in the fifth trumpet judgment that these locusts were commanded not to harm the grass of the earth (Revelation 9:4). If there wasn't any grass because it had been burned up in the first judgment then these locusts would not have this command in the fifth judgment. Sound simplistic? You have to remember this book is not information, but a revelation! It must be spiritually discerned and that's why you must study it for yourself in the Holy Spirit. The entirety of Scripture must be taken into account; otherwise, if you live in America this book will be looked at through the non-discerning, blinded eyes of western society and culture.

3) Revelation 8:13 is a key to why I believe the first four judgments are only fulfilled within the sixth trumpet

judgment. *"I looked, and I heard an angel flying though the midst of heaven, saying with a loud voice, 'Woe, woe, woe to the inhabitants of the earth, **because of the remaining blasts of the trumpet of the three angels who are about to sound** (fifth, sixth, and seventh trumpet judgments)!'"* (emphasis mine) Doesn't this statement indicate that the first four were not woes but warnings? I would think that the first four trumpet judgments would be woes as well. When we look at the first four isn't it obvious that if they were to happen, we would see mass destruction over the entire earth?

- A third of the earth and trees and all green grass burned up!
- A third of the sea became blood and a third of the creatures in the sea died as well as a third of the ships destroyed!
- A third of the waters of rivers and springs became wormwood! And many men died because of the water!
- A third of the sun, moon, and stars were darkened and a third of the day and night did not shine!

We see in the sixth judgment that a third of mankind was killed by these four angels. The key words within the first four judgments is also in the sixth: **a third**. If a third of all the destruction that was pronounced in the first four were carried out, we would have mass chaos and destruction over the entire earth. Look at what happened in Japan when the tsunami hit in 2011. Houses, buildings, cars, and ships smashed all together. There was close to 20,000 lives lost that day. The smell of death was probably overwhelming. Mass destruction on a small and remote section of the island of Japan. Not even close to a third of the ships destroyed in the second trumpet judgment. This alone would be a woe on the earth if it happened! California is known for wild fires and consuming thousands of acres of trees and brush, yet it's just a dent in the state of California. Not even close to a third of all the earth and trees being burned up. Then we see massive fish die-offs. Millions have just died for no apparent reason, yet not even close to a third of the living creatures in the sea dying. Are you beginning to see what these first four would accomplish on the earth if they were to happen? We would smell the stench and experience the devastation. Are these things that have happened in Japan or California, and the fish die-offs, etc.; just a shadow of the things that are to come on the earth?

CHAPTER 7

THE FIRST WOE

THE FIFTH TRUMPET JUDGMENT

"Then the fifth angel sounded: And I saw a star fallen from heaven to the earth." Revelation 9:1

Is this star that has fallen from heaven to the earth one of the manifestations talked about in the sign which is recorded in Revelation 12:9? *"So the great dragon was cast out* (of heaven), *that serpent of old, called the Devil and Satan, who deceives the whole world; he was cast to the earth, and his angels were cast out with him."* Revelation 6:13 says, *"The stars of heaven fell to the earth."* This is one of those stars. Only this star **was given** the key to the bottomless pit. Once again I must ask the question: "Who gave him the key?" The Scripture goes on to say that with this key -- *". . . he opened the bottomless pit and smoke arose out of the pit like the smoke of a great furnace. So the sun and the air were darkened* *because of the smoke of the pit. Then out of the smoke locusts came upon the earth. And to them was given power, as the scorpions of the earth have power."* (Revelation 9:2-3)

GMO BUGS!?

What is the power of a scorpion? Their sting. I believe these are GMO bugs that are released on the earth. They are not released over all the earth, but in the Middle East and surrounding areas. The reason I believe this is because they were commanded only to harm those who do not have the seal of God on their foreheads. This command would mean that there would be those who have the seal of God on their foreheads. Those that had the seal were Jews from all twelve tribes which would most likely be in Israel at the time.

These GMO bugs were not commanded to kill these men, but only to torment them. Let me ask a question: When a hornet flies around your head or neck what do you do? How do you respond? It's not hard to imagine what life would be like with these creatures around for 5 months. Five months is the average life span of a desert locust.[1] What is described in the fifth seal is not symbolic although the description of them is, as we will see below. These creatures were commanded not to harm the grass or any green thing. Only bugs of this nature eat green things. The ability of genetically modifying bugs is a very real possibility in this day and age that we live in.[2] The genes from a scorpion could be taken and forced into the DNA of a locust. Billions of these little creatures have plagued these areas since Israel was freed from Pharaoh in Egypt. We see in Exodus 10 the plague of locusts that came upon Egypt and all the territory of Egypt. Moses describes this plague in Exodus 10:5-6, *"They shall cover the face of the earth, so that no one will be able to see the earth; and they shall eat the residue of what is left, which remains to you from the hail, and they shall eat every tree which grows up for you out of the field. They shall fill your houses, the houses of all your servants, and the houses of all the Egyptians."* It

---

[1] https://en.wikipedia.org/wiki/Desert_locust
[2] http://tv.greenmedinfo.com/what-is-a-gmo-explained-in-1-minute/

74

says in verse 14, *"They were very severe; previously there had been no such locusts as they, nor shall there be such after them."* When they are given stingers like scorpions and commanded to harm men, we will see the first "woe" released upon this earth. There will never be another plague like this one ever again! Joel gives the description of the locusts of his day in Joel 1:6, *"His teeth are the teeth of a lion"* which parallels with Revelation 9:8, *"Their teeth were like lions teeth."* Again in Joel 2:4, *"Their appearance is like the appearance of horses"* paralleled with Revelation 9:7, *"The shape of the locusts was like horses prepared for battle",* also Joel 2:5 paralleled with Revelation 9:9, *"With a noise like chariots"* and *"the sound of their wings was like the sound of chariots with many horses running into battle."* The only difference between those mentioned in Joel and those mentioned in Revelation is: *"On their heads were crowns of something like gold, and their faces were like faces of men"* (Revelation 9:7). I see a crown as representing rulership or dominance. The face of a man will exhibit the intent of the man; in this case to inflict harm. *"They had hair like women's hair"* (Revelation 9:8, of which I have no clue). Revelation 9:9, *"They had breastplates like breastplates of iron."* I take this to mean that they are hard to kill. The fact that there will be so many of them you wouldn't want to attempt to kill them anyway. This plague will be so horrific that men will seek death as it says in 9:6. They will desire to die, and death will flee from them.

DESTRUCTION VS DESTROYER

The last statement from the fifth trumpet judgment is in verse 11 which says, *"They* (the locusts) *had as king over them the angel of the bottomless pit, whose name in Hebrew is Abaddon* (meaning destruction), *but in Greek he has the name Apollyon* (meaning destroyer)." The definition of destruction is "the state or fact of being destroyed;" which would mean those on the receiving end. The definition of destroyer is "one that destroys;" meaning the giver of destruction. Since the Hebrew language is affiliated with Israel and Greek would be affiliated with western cultures, does this mean that Israel is the receiver of destruction and western cultures are the giver?

One woe is past. Behold, still two more woes are coming after these things. These woes are also under the seventh seal and must be broken off the scroll.

THE SECOND WOE
The Sixth Trumpet Judgment
"So the four angels, who had been prepared for the hour and day and month and year, were released to kill a third of mankind.'
Revelation 9:15

As I mentioned earlier in this chapter, there is a thread that ties the first four judgments together with this one. The words "a third." This judgment is the second woe that is mentioned in Revelation 8:13. *"Woe, **woe**, woe to the inhabitants of the earth!"* It is most important that we look at this "woe" with the loving, merciful, gracious eyes of the Father upon us, lest we be overwhelmed beyond words. Again, we see the words "golden altar" written. The last mention of the golden altar was in Revelation 8:3 were the angel was offering incense with the prayers of all the saints on it. Now we see that there is a voice coming from the four horns of the golden altar saying, *"Release the four angels who are bound at the great river Euphrates"* (9:14). These are the same four that were told to not harm the earth till the 144,000 were sealed (7:1-3). If you look on a map of the Middle East you will find that the Euphrates River flows right up through Iraq and Syria. At this present time, ISIS (Islamic State of Iraq and Syria) is invading and controlling large portions of these two countries. They have one mandate: To see Islam as the controlling, dominate religion throughout the entire earth. Just east of Iraq is Iran, who has the same mandate for the world. Iran is mentioned in the book of Daniel as Persia (Daniel 10:13,20), and also in Jeremiah 49:34-36 as Elam. Elam was what is presently called the Iranian plateau. Iran is also alluded to in Revelation 16:12 as the kings from the east; east of the Euphrates River. The two sects (mentioned above) are Shiite and Sunni, which are very similar, but have different ideas of who should proceed Mohammad, who was Islam's prophet and is highly respected by

76

both groups. ISIS or Iraq is Sunni[3] and Iran is Shiite[4] and they are at odds with each other. Iran is in the process of obtaining a Nuclear bomb (if they haven't already obtained it). That being said brings significance to this woe which comes from the Euphrates River and kills a third of all mankind (*"Release the four angels that are bound at the great Euphrates River."* (Revelation 9:14) This happening today would mean 2.3 billion people would die. Overwhelming? Yes, very much so! This is why we must keep our eyes on Jesus. You will notice in Revelation 9:16 the words, *"Now the number of the army of the horsemen was two hundred million; I heard the number of them."* In other words John, at the beginning of the Revelation, saw only four horsemen in the first four seals that were broken off. Now he hears the number two hundred million. Wow! The number had grown to an alarming number. As the horsemen were connected to judgment upon Jerusalem in Zechariah 1:8-12, so will the two hundred million horsemen be connected with judgment upon the world. My own thoughts on this bring connection to the incense offered with the saint's prayers who are under the altar (Revelation 8:3) and the angel throwing fire to the earth (Revelation 8:5) and then the voice from the four horns of the golden altar before God releasing the four angels to kill a third of mankind (Revelation 9:13-15). Is what we see here, the avenging of the blood of all the souls under the altar? All the souls from the blood of Abel to the blood of those shed up to the Day of the Lord!

NUCLEAR?

We find the description of these horses and horsemen in Revelation 9:17-19. *"And thus I saw the horses in the vision: those who sat on them had breastplates of fiery red, hyacinth blue, and sulfur yellow."* You will notice that the color description of the breastplates is the very color of fire; hot fire! *"And the heads of the horses were like the heads of lions; and out of their mouths came fire, smoke, and brimstone. By these three plagues a third of mankind was killed -- by the fire and the smoke and the brimstone which came out of their mouths."* This sounds like a nuclear

---

[3]https://en.wikipedia.org/wiki/Islamic_State_of_Iraq_and_the_Levant
[4]https://en.wikipedia.org/wiki/Islam_in_Iran

explosion. It could be one explosion or most likely several explosions at once or at various intervals. Either way, we see the preparation for this as counted down to the exact hour, day, month, and year. It took preparation and the precise execution of this event. The description written in verse 19 seems to be in addition with the fire, smoke, and brimstone coming out of the horses mouths: *"For their power is in their mouths and in their tails; for their tails are like serpents, having heads; and with them they do harm."* Amplified puts it this way, *"Their tails are like serpents, for they have heads, and it is by means of them that **they wound people**."* (emphasis mine) People are not killed by the tails, they are just wounded. I believe this speaks of nuclear fallout on other parts of the world. There is much documentation on the results of nuclear fallout and how it effects people[5]

The results of this on the world brought no change in the people who survived. Notice verses 20 and 21: *"But the rest of mankind, who were not killed by these plagues, **did not repent** of the works of their hands, that they should not worship demons, and idols of gold, silver, brass, stone, and wood, which can neither see nor hear nor walk. And they **did not repent** of their murders or their sorceries or their sexual immorality or their thefts."* (emphasis mine)

After a third of mankind is killed with major results of the stench of death and destruction throughout the entire earth, the rest of mankind carried on as if nothing had happened. They ate and drank and carried on without repentance. You would like to think that some would have realized the magnitude of this as coming from God, yet it's God who points out (ahead of time) that they **did not repent**. This has similarity to what it looked like in Genesis 6:5, *"Then the Lord saw that the wickedness of man was great in the earth, and that every intent of the thoughts of his heart was only evil continually."* So the Lord destroyed all men by flooding the earth and starting over. It was not a failure to Him, but a restart because the earth was corrupt and filled with violence. The Lord said to Noah, *"Make yourself an ark . . . everything that is on the earth shall die. But I will establish My covenant with you."* (Genesis 6:14-18)

---

[5] https://en.wikipedia.org/wiki/Effects_of_nuclear_explosions_on_human_health

CONSIDER THIS:

February 4, 2015 6AM (I trembled when I saw this!): The four angels in chapter 7 that were commanded or bound from harming the earth **until** the 144,000 were sealed are the same four angels in chapter 9 that are released to kill a third of mankind. In chapter 8:6 it says the seven angels who had the seven trumpets "prepared themselves" to sound. The first four were being "prepared". The last three are proclaimed as "woes" upon the earth. Under the sixth trumpet, "the second woe," these four angels (after being prepared) were released. Only a nuclear explosion could kill 2.3 billion people (a third of mankind). Its no wonder there was hail with fire following mixed with blood! When nuclear explosions happen, man is vaporized as in Zechariah 14:12. Their flesh shall dissolve while they stand on their feet. A third of the trees were burned. A third of the sea became blood and a third of the sea creatures died. A third of ships destroyed. A third of rivers and springs became bitter wormwood. A third of the sun, moon, and stars darkened so a third of day and night did not shine.

I believe as the 144,000 are being sealed, that these angels are being prepared for this day. Hatred for the Jews, Christians, and the west is mounting to a level as never before in history. The sign that will be most evident to all mankind before this day happens is the releasing of hordes of locusts that sting like scorpions. They are **only** commanded to harm those who have not been sealed on their foreheads. In other words, the 144,000 will not be harmed. The killing of a third of mankind will usher in the beast and his system.

CHAPTER 8

THE SECOND COMING!

"Now as He sat on the Mount of Olives, the disciples came to Him privately, saying, 'Tell us, when will these things be? And what will be the sign of Your coming (**the Rapture?**)*, and of the end of the age?'"* Matthew 24:3

I must take the opportunity to address the second coming of Jesus before continuing on in the second woe. Jesus begins to address these things with His disciples. He starts out by warning them (and us) to not be deceived. Which indicates there would be a strong possibility in the last days of His followers actually becoming deceived. The way that Jesus addresses this is somewhat puzzling. He says there will be many that will come in His name! They are saying, "I am the Christ, the Anointed one of God!" (Christ means anointed one)[6] They come **in His name** believing that they are anointed by God and end up deceiving people. Sad to say that there are preachers, teachers, prophets, evangelists, and pastors who claim His name and have an anointing, yet walk in darkness. We as His Church need Holy Spirit discernment most desperately in these last days! This very thing would parallel with Matthew 7:21-23: *"Not everyone who says to Me, 'Lord, Lord,' shall enter the kingdom of heaven, but he who does the will of My Father in heaven. Many will say to Me in that day, 'Lord, Lord, have we not prophesied in Your name, cast out demons in Your name, and done many wonders in Your name?' And then I will declare to them, 'I never knew you; depart from Me, you who practice lawlessness!' "* (emphasis mine) The people addressed here are "anointed(?)" to cast out demons, prophesy, and do many miracles; yet they are lawless and are deceiving many people into thinking that they are of God. I love what Mike Bickle says every time he gives a teaching. He tells those he is teaching to not just believe what he says, but to study it and make sure the teaching is of God. Most people don't study, so they just receive whatever the "man of God" says.

Jesus continues by describing what it will be like in the last days: *"Wars, nations rising, famines, pestilences, earthquakes, tribulation, hatred, betrayal, false prophets (deception), lawlessness and love growing cold; the gospel preached and then the end will come"* (Matthew 24:6-14). He continues in verse 15 with the word *"therefore"*. As Bob Mumford used to say, "When you see the word 'therefore,' look to see what it is there for." Jesus is referring to what He had just said. *"**Therefore** when you see the abomination of desolation, standing in the holy place . . ."* (emphasis mine) This will happen in the midst of and during all the turmoil (mentioned above) that will be going on in the world. Jesus then addresses His followers who will be living in these days: *"Then let those who are in Judea flee to the mountains. Let him who is on the housetop not go down to take anything out of his house. And let him who is in the field not go back to get his clothes. But woe to those who are pregnant and to those who are nursing babies in those days! And pray that your flight may not be in winter or on the Sabbath. For*

---

[6] https://en.wikipedia.org/wiki/Christ

83

then there will be great tribulation, such as has not been since the beginning of the world until this time, no, nor ever shall be. And unless those days were shortened, no flesh would be saved; but for **the elect's** *sake those days will be shortened"* (Matthew 24:16-22 - emphasis mine). It sounds like all hell is being unleashed upon the earth at this time. Up to this point, Jesus has not addressed His disciples question nor made any reference to His coming. He tells them at this point that these are only the beginning of sorrows. Jesus is making them aware that many sorrows are coming! To those who strictly adhere to the positive confession, Jesus just made a very negative one. You have to understand that He loves His people extremely and desires their love in return. He saw what was coming upon the earth and wanted His people to be ready to stand in the face of many sorrows. We must be careful that we don't take on the attitude of the great harlot of Revelation 18:7 who says in her heart, *"I sit as queen, and am no widow, and* **will not see sorrow***!"* (emphasis mine)

He continues by warning that false Christ's and false prophets will show great signs and wonders to deceive, if possible, even the elect. **His people are still on the earth at this time**. Then Jesus describes to His people (us, the church) what His coming will look like. *"For as the lightning comes from the east and flashes to the west, so also will the coming of the Son of Man be"* (Matthew 24:27). He then says in verse 29, *"**Immediately after** the tribulation of **those days** the sun will be darkened, and the moon will not give its light; the stars will fall from heaven, and the powers of the heavens will be shaken."* (emphasis mine) Please give notice to what Jesus then says in verse 30: *"**Then** the sign of the Son of Man will appear in heaven."* After all the turmoil, devastation, and deception is released, Jesus returns in the clouds! Verse 30-31 continues, *"And then all the tribes of the earth will mourn, and they will see the Son of Man coming on the clouds of heaven with power and great glory. And He will send His angels with a great sound of a trumpet, and they will gather together His elect from the four winds, from one end of heaven to the other."* What I am about to say will probably shock some of you. Again, I ask that you study all these things for yourself. Don't accept or reject what I am about to say without looking into it diligently for yourself. I don't see anywhere in the

Scriptures where the Church (God's elect) suddenly disappear from the earth as if like a magic trick. The rapture is portrayed this way in videos that you will find on Youtube[7]. I will be very careful when I address this, because I had believed this way for many, many years; since becoming a Christian in the fall of 1971. I did not change my mind because someone told me different. It has come through countless hours of study and searching the Scriptures for understanding of the last days. As I studied, I would look very intently for Scriptural evidence of the rapture so that I could know when it would take place. I will give my evidence from Scriptures for what I believe, and you must find your own evidence for what you believe. Paul talks about Jesus' return in 2 Thessalonians 2:1-4; *"Now, brethren, concerning the coming of our Lord Jesus Christ and our gathering together to Him . . . let no one deceive you by any means; for that Day will not come unless the falling away comes first, and the man of sin* (lawlessness) *is revealed, the son of perdition, who opposes and exalts himself above all that is called God or that is worshipped, so that he sits as God in the temple of God, showing himself that he is God."* Paul says Jesus will not come back until the "abomination of desolation" is standing in the holy place, as mentioned by Jesus in Matthew 24:15. What Paul says is in agreement with what Jesus says. There are Scriptures that many use which seem to support the rapture. One is found in 1 Corinthians 15:51-52 were Paul says, *"Behold, I tell you a mystery: We shall not all sleep, but we shall all be changed--in a moment, in the twinkling of an eye, at the last trumpet. For the trumpet will sound, and the dead will be raised incorruptible, and we shall be changed."* I don't believe that this supports the "rapture" as portrayed in the video mentioned above. In 1 Corinthians 15, Paul is presenting evidence for the resurrection and giving hope to those who have seen loved ones die in the Lord. He says, *"If Christ has not risen, then faith is futile and those who have died in Christ have been lost forever."* (verses 17-18) These people needed assurance that their loved ones were going to be resurrected when He comes back. He explains in verses 12-18, 29, 35-36, and 41-54 that Christ did indeed rise from the dead and those who have died in Christ will rise also. The words "dead, died, die, and asleep" appear 26 times in this

---

[7] http://www.youtube.com/watch?v=VyzaJfRSLts

85

chapter alone. How we will be changed is the mystery Paul speaks of in verse 51: *"Behold, I tell you a mystery: we shall not all sleep* (die), *but we shall all be changed* (as Paul describes in verses 35-50). In verse 52 he says, *"We are changed in the twinkling of an eye, at the last trumpet."* Is the last trumpet recorded in Matthew 24:31? *"He will send His angels with a great sound of a **trumpet**, and they will gather together His elect!"*

THE LAST TRUMPET

What is the last trumpet, and who will sound it? The trumpet was sounded in Exodus 19 on the mountain of Sinai. *"Then it came to pass on the third day, in the morning, that there were thunderings and lightnings and a thick cloud on the mountain; and the sound of the trumpet was very loud, so that all the people who were in the camp trembled."* Was this just the sound of a trumpet or something else that sounded like a trumpet? If we look in 1 Thessalonians 4:16, we see the Lord (Himself) descending from heaven; *"For the Lord Himself will descend from heaven with a shout, with the voice of an archangel, and with the trumpet of God."* His voice alone, when He shouts, will sound like an archangel; like the trumpet of God! Remember, He is a man who has been given glorified power from God. He has been exalted above every name that at His name all knees will bow. In Zephaniah, we see the mention of the trumpet and also the day of the Lord, which is mentioned throughout his book. This seems to be referring to a day in the future because of verses like *"I will consume everything . . . I will consume man and beast . . . I will consume the birds, the fish, and all stumbling blocks along with the wicked. The great day of the Lord is near; It is near and hastens quickly. The noise of the day of the Lord is bitter; there the mighty men shall cry out. That day is a day of wrath, trouble, distress, devastation, darkness, gloominess . . . a day of **trumpet** and **alarm**."* (Zephaniah 1:2,3,14-16 - emphasis mine) You will find every one of these things just mentioned, in the book of Revelation.

We see in Revelation 4:1-2, a snapshot likened to the change in regard to the twinkling of an eye as described in 1 Corinthians 15:52, *"After these things I looked, and behold, a door standing open* *in heaven. And the first voice which I heard was like a **trumpet** speaking with me, saying, 'Come up here, and I will show you things which must take place after this.' **Immediately I was in the Spirit**."* (emphasis mine) John was immediately in the Spirit (in the twinkling of an eye). He was changed immediately at the trumpet sound which was the voice of Jesus. John, as he was flesh and blood, could not be caught up into heaven unless he was in the Spirit. He had to be changed. We see this change not just in 1 Corinthians 15:52, but also in 1 Thessalonians 4:13-17 were Paul is addressing the same thing that he addressed in the Corinthian Church concerning those who had died and if they would be resurrected. *"But I do not want you to be ignorant, brethren, concerning those who have fallen asleep, lest you sorrow as others who have no hope. For if we believe that Jesus died and rose again, even so God will bring with Him those **who sleep** in Jesus. For this we say to you by the word of the Lord, that we who are alive and remain until the coming of the Lord will by no means precede those **who are asleep**. For the Lord Himself will descend from heaven with a shout, with the voice of an archangel, and with the trumpet of God. And **the dead** in Christ will rise first. Then we who are alive and remain shall be caught up together with them in the clouds to meet the Lord in the air. And thus we shall always be with the Lord. **Therefore comfort one another with these words.**"* (emphasis mine) There were those who were sorrowful because they thought their loved ones who had died would not be resurrected. Paul is proclaiming hope to those who had loved ones die before Jesus came back. They will be resurrected first before those that remain alive. All these will be caught up in the clouds when the last trumpet sounds.

The only evidence that I find of a possible "rapture" is in Revelation 14:14-16, *"Then I looked, and behold, a white cloud, and on the cloud sat One like the Son of Man, having on His head a golden crown, and in His hand a sharp sickle. And another angel came out of the temple, crying with a loud voice to Him who sat on the cloud, 'Thrust in Your sickle and reap, for the time has come for You to reap, for the harvest of the earth is ripe.' So He who sat on the cloud thrust in His sickle on the earth, and the earth was reaped."* John had a revelation of Jesus on a cloud and an angel telling Him its time to reap. This indicates that the Father sends the angel to Jesus to tell Him it's time. This would confirm Mark 13:32 where Jesus says, *"But of that day and hour **no one knows**, not even the angels in heaven, **nor the Son**, but only the Father."* (emphasis mine) We see in Revelation that the Father has sent the angel from the temple to deliver the message to the Son who sits on the cloud, *"Thrust in Your sickle and reap!"* Immediately after Jesus reaps the earth, another angel comes out of the temple also having a sharp sickle. He is told by an angel who came out from the **altar** having power over fire to gather the clusters of the vine. Please notice that he came out from the altar. There has been much activity around the altar up to this point (souls crying out from under the altar - Revelation 6:9-10). So he gathered the vine and threw it into the winepress of the wrath of God (Revelation 14:17-20). *"Blood came out of the winepress up to the horses bridles."* So we see the righteous and the wicked reaped at the same time. This would coincide with Matthew 13:24-30 and 36-43 in the parable of the wheat and tares. *"The Son of Man will send out His angels, and they will gather out of His kingdom all things that offend, and those who practice lawlessness, and will cast them into the furnace of fire. There will be wailing and gnashing of teeth. Then the righteous will shine forth as the sun in the kingdom of their Father."* (verses 41-43) If the first reaping by Jesus is the "rapture," then it happens at the end of the age.

TWO MONKEY WRENCHES

And now I will throw a "monkey wrench" into this. Revelation 20:4-6 mentions those who had been beheaded for not worshipping the beast. It says, *"They lived and reigned with Christ for a thousand years. But the rest of the dead did not live again until the thousand years were finished. This is **the first resurrection**."* (emphasis mine) This Scripture just said it was the first resurrection! If this is the first resurrection (those beheaded), then the resurrection that Paul mentions in 1 Thessalonians 4:16; *"The dead in Christ will rise first"* is not going to happen until after the thousand years is up. If there is a first resurrection, it only stands to reason there will be a second resurrection. Only it will happen at the end of the age. I must throw one more "monkey wrench" into this mix. In Revelation 7:9-17, John sees a great multitude which could not be numbered clothed in white. The sight was so great that all the angels, the 24

88

elders and the four living creatures fell on their faces and worshipped God! One of the elders said to John, *"Who are these arrayed in white robes, and where did they come from?"* The answer that the elder gave to John is most revealing. *"These are the ones who come out of the great tribulation!"* (verse 14) I would love more than anything to be "raptured" before all hell breaks loose during or before this tribulation, but I don't see evidence of this in Scripture. Sorry! Again, please study it and prove that I have been mistaken, for some who are well known and of prominent position in ministry have accused me and others who believe this way of being a false prophet. You must decide for yourself! Jesus is coming, but we can't build a doctrine on one or two Scriptures. We must take the whole of Scripture to establish the truth. Peter addresses something worth pointing out in regard to the day of the Lord. II Peter 3 talks of Jesus' coming and the attitudes of those who have become disillusioned. Peter describes what the day of the Lord will look like in verses 10-13. *"The day of the Lord will come as a thief in the night, in which the heavens will pass away with a great noise, and the elements will melt with fervent heat; both the earth and the works that are in it will be burned up. Therefore, since all these things will be dissolved, what manner of persons ought you to be in holy conduct and godliness looking for and hastening the coming of the day of God . . . Nevertheless, we, according to His promise, look for new heavens and a new earth in which righteousness dwells."* Then Peter, in verse 14, addresses saints throughout all of history when he says, *"Therefore, beloved, looking forward to these things be diligent to be found by Him in peace, without spot and blameless."* He then speaks of Paul who also speaks of these things in his epistles. Peter says, *"there are some things hard to understand which untaught and unstable people twist to their own destruction, as they do also the rest of Scriptures"* (verse 16). I also find some things in Paul's epistles hard to understand; yet what Peter is addressing is the fact that some people who haven't done their homework go off half-cocked and spread what they think is sound teaching. He says they are unstable. Does the word "unstable" mean mentally ill or is Paul saying they don't have a solid scriptural foundation to speak from so they speak and teach lies and ignorant half-truths? People who are mentally ill are very obvious; but those that are unstable speak and present themselves as scholars. This is why Peter exhorts all believers in verse 18, *"But grow in grace and knowledge of our Lord and Savior Jesus Christ."* **HE KNOWS THOSE WHO KNOW HIM!**

> *"DO NOT let your hearts be troubled (distressed, agitated). You believe in and adhere to and trust in and rely on God; believe in and adhere to and trust in and rely also on Me. In My Father's house there are many dwelling places (homes). If it were not so, I would have told you; for I am going away to prepare a place for you. And when (if) I go and make ready a place for you, I will come back again and will take you to Myself, that where I am you may be also. And [to the place] where I am going, you know the way. Thomas said to Him, Lord,* **we do not know where You are going***, so how can we know the way?*** (John 14:1-4 AMP - emphasis mine)

Would it be fair to say that all of us, like Thomas, have asked that question: "We do not know where You have gone, so how can we know the way?" We know that Jesus was lifted off of the earth and ascended into heaven, but where He went is actually a mystery. We could quote Scriptures that say He went to heaven and sat down at the right hand of the Father, which is true. We could quote Scriptures that say He is interceding for us, which is true. We could speculate many things regarding where He is and what He is doing, but we don't really have a clue; or do we? Jesus' response to Thomas is compelling; *"I am the way, the truth, and the life. No one comes to the Father except through Me."* (John 14:6) This same verse could be read this way: *"I* (the slain Lamb pictured throughout the book of Revelation) *am the way, the truth, and the life."* Jesus is pictured throughout the entire book of Revelation as the slain Lamb. Being married to the Lamb is God's mandate as Revelation 19:7 says, *"Let us be glad and rejoice and give Him glory, for the marriage of the Lamb has come, and His wife has made herself ready."*

We have an all conclusive need to be related to and connected with the Father! It is His very words to us that affirm us and make us His sons and daughters. It's only through our intimacy with the Father that Jesus can say to us in the end, "I know you!" "I

see in your eyes that you have been with My Father and know Him!"
Dwelling in intimacy (in the secret place) with the Father through
Holy Spirit is the only place we will truly understand and know what
is on His heart. The entire Bible is filled with His words! As we
read and diligently pursue (in study through Jesus Christ) the very
words that God has given through all His prophets and messengers,
we will understand the very heart of God---His purposes and plans.
Heaven will become a place where we will dwell and not just visit
once in a while.

CONSIDER THIS:

Heir or Arrogance?

*"Now I say that **the heir**, as long as he is a child, does not differ at all from a slave, though **he is master of all** . . . God has sent the Spirit of His Son into our hearts . . . Therefore we are no longer a slave, but a son, and if a son, then an heir."* Galatians 4:1-7 (emphasis mine)

An heir is the master of all because he is an heir of God. If we have the Spirit of Jesus in us, then we will be like Jesus and have what Jesus has. This would confirm what Hebrews 2:5-8 says, *"He has not put the world to come, of which we speak, in subjection to angels, but one testified in a certain place, saying, 'What is man that You are mindful of him? You have made him a little lower than the angels . . . and set him over the works of Your hands. You have put **all things** in subjection under his feet.' "* (emphasis mine) This would mean that God has made us an heir to His throne! (Heir or Arrogance?) To confirm this notion we will look at Revelation 3:21, *"To him who overcomes I will grant to sit with Me on My throne, as I also overcame and sat down with My Father on His throne."* This says very plainly that an heir has to be an overcomer. Does that mean if someone does not overcome in an area of their life that they will not be an heir? Even more it says in Revelation 2:11, *"He who overcomes shall not be hurt by the second death."* Does this mean if someone does not overcome in an area of their life that they will be hurt by the second death? Jesus looks for relationship. Sons have relationship with their father. If sons, then heirs; how could it be any different? Jesus just promised that we could sit, not just on His throne, but also on the Father's throne. We must note that immediately after this promise in Revelation 3:21, we see in Revelation 4 the description of a throne set in heaven, and One sat on the throne. This picture of the reigning, all powerful, beautiful and awesome God of the universe is described in a most glorious fashion! Stop right here and read it! This God has promised to us, His heirs (His overcomers), that we will rule and reign with Him over the universe! Over all the world! Over all nations, tribes, peoples and tongues! I pray that this will sink into our spirits! As Jesus has said many times, *"He who has ears to hear let him hear!"*

CHAPTER 9

THE SECOND WOE CONTINUED

THE SIXTH TRUMPET JUDGMENT

We left off in Chapter 7 with a third of mankind being killed. I don't think our minds can comprehend the magnitude of this happening in the world. We understand what happens in our nation when something like 9/11 happens, which is only a microcosm compared to a third of mankind be killed. This happening today would equate to 2.3 billion people being killed since the population of the world is 7 billion. What would happen to the world's economy in an event like this? What would be the dominating aroma throughout the entire earth? The stench of death would be everywhere! Does this sound unbelievable to you? I decided to address the second coming in the middle of the second woe because of the magnitude of its destruction. If we go through the tribulation before we are raptured, then this will be a major part of it! Again, I ask, please study for yourself. This major life changing event is the introduction to the next events that happen in and surrounding Israel from Revelation chapters 10-13. Although it looks very bleak, I see something preceding these events that is most glorious in chapter 10:1-8. Jesus will have all enemies put under His feet!!

THE "LITTLE" BOOK
Revelation 10:1-3, 5-8

*"I saw still another mighty angel coming down from heaven, clothed with a cloud. And a rainbow was on his head, his face was like the sun, and his feet like pillars of fire. He had a **little** book open in his hand. And he set his **right foot** on the **sea** and his **left foot** on the **land**, and cried with a loud voice, as when a lion roars. The angel whom I saw standing on the **sea** and on the **land** raised up his hand to heaven and swore by Him who lives forever and ever, who created heaven and the things that are in it, the earth and the things that are in it, and the sea and the things that are in it, that there should be delay no longer, but in the days of the sounding of the seventh angel, when he is about to sound, the mystery of God would be finished, as He declared to His servants the prophets. Then the voice which I heard from heaven spoke to me again and said, 'Go, take the **little** book which is open in the hand of the angel **who stands on** the **sea** and on the **earth**."* (emphasis mine)

If you will notice the Scripture makes reference to the "little" book open in his hand and it points out twice that this angel is standing on the sea and land. Then there is a voice from heaven which makes reference to the "little" book open and the fact that the angel is standing on the sea and on the earth. I must point out that God does not waste His words! What is pointed out in this portion of Scripture is of utmost importance to us who believe. Before I explain, I would like to make reference to two Scriptures. The first one is in 1 Corinthians 15:25, *"For He must reign till He has put all enemies under His feet."* And the second is in Hebrews 10:12-13: *"But this Man, after He had offered one sacrifice for sins forever, sat down at the right hand of God, from that time waiting till His enemies are made His footstool"* You might ask, "What do these Scriptures have to do with standing on the sea and earth?" If we look ahead at what is coming in Revelation 13, we will see how this relates. Verse 1: *"Then I stood on the sand of the sea. And I saw a beast rising up out of the sea . . . "* (emphasis mine) In verse 11: *"Then I saw another beast coming up out of the earth . . . "*(emphasis mine) The angel is **standing on the sea and earth** making the Lord's enemies His footstool! **They are under His feet!** Wow! What happens in chapters 10-13 is the prophetic word John proclaims after he eats the "little" book open in the hand of the angel. A "little" book can be read quickly. John eats it and it is sweet as honey in his mouth, but makes his stomach bitter. This is a bittersweet moment for John. You will notice in Revelation 11 and 12 a reference is given to a three and one-half year period (just a blip of time), which is mentioned four times in these two chapters. One is in regard to the trampling of the Jerusalem by the Gentiles (11:2), another is in regard to the two witnesses prophesying (11:3), and the other two references are in regard to the great sign of the woman clothed with the sun, with the moon under her feet, and a garland of twelve stars on her head (12:1,6,14). The bitter is in chapter 13:5 in regard to the beast, *"He was given authority to continue for forty-two months* (three and one-half years)." You have to remember that all of this from chapters 11 through 13 takes place after a third of mankind is killed. Why is it that America is called the great Satan by Muslim nations? Also there is a growing hatred from Muslim nations towards many nations in Europe who are endeavoring not to comply with Islam's agenda and the spread of Sharia law throughout the world. Israel is looked at as pigs by Muslim nations and has been threatened with destruction times without number. Are we looking at the beginning of what is recorded in Revelation 13 regarding the reign of the beast?

THE MYSTERY OF GOD

The angel that is standing on the sea and the earth makes a loud proclamation: *"**In the days of the sounding of the seventh angel**, when he is about to sound, **the mystery of God would be finished**, as He declared to His servants the prophets"* (Revelation 10:7

- emphasis mine). God has a mystery. A mystery that will be finished or completed at and during the sound of the seventh trumpet. This Scripture mentions that the mystery has been declared to His servants the prophets. Some would compulsively say right here that the mystery is Jesus revealed in and through the prophets. Yes, but if you study the prophets there is so much more that has not been revealed concerning Jesus and the plan He desires for Jerusalem, Israel, and the earth. One such place is in Isaiah chapter 61 starting in verse 3 and proceeding through chapter 66. This continues after what Jesus had proclaimed concerning Himself in Isaiah 61:1-2, *"The Spirit of the Lord God is upon Me . . . "* I will not expound on this portion of Isaiah because of the enormous quantity of references to the future. To expound on this would take books to explain. I will only say that you must study this for yourself. Jesus is revealed throughout Isaiah to a nation that made a love covenant with God, but refuses to live according to that covenant. He was prophesied to Israel and the world several decades before that night in Bethlehem. When we read what happens after the seventh angel sounds, we see the wrap up stages beginning to happen (the mystery of God finished). Notice what the twenty-four elders proclaim in Revelation 11:15-18:

> *"Then the seventh angel sounded: And there were loud voices in heaven, saying, 'The kingdoms of this world have become the kingdoms of our Lord and of His Christ, and He shall reign forever and ever!' And the twenty-four elders who sat before God on their thrones fell on their faces and worshiped God, saying:*
>
> *"We give You thanks, O Lord God Almighty,*
> *The One who is and who was and who is to come,*
> *Because You have taken Your great power and reigned.*
> *The nations were angry, and Your wrath has come, and the time of the dead, that they should be judged, and that You should reward Your servants the prophets and the saints, and those who fear Your name, small and great, and should destroy those who destroy the earth.' "*

After this proclamation, God the Father put His signature on it; *"The temple of God was opened in heaven, and the ark of His covenant was seen in His temple. And there were lightnings, noises, thunderings, and earthquake, and great hail."* We have to realize that the Jews were not suppose to ever see inside the temple (especially the ark) or they would be struck dead immediately. However the Scripture said that the temple was opened and the ark seen. God opened it up! God put His ark on display! I believe what happens in chapters 11 and 12 is related to the Jews in Israel. The temple opened and the ark seen would have significant meaning to Jews. We know that the veil of the temple was torn when Jesus died which gives us continuous access to the presence of God. The temple opened and the ark seen is something that we cannot take lightly. Nor can we walk in pride thinking we are more special to God than the Jews who were called to be His people from the very beginning.

THE TWO WITNESSES

As we look into this, it must be pointed out again that this takes place in Israel, specifically Jerusalem; and, is still part of the second woe. Verse 2 of chapter 11 mentions the holy city and verse 7 mentions the great city where the Lord was crucified. I cannot emphasize this enough that this takes place after a third of mankind is killed. In verse 1 of chapter 11, we see John was given a reed for a measuring rod. He was told to measure the temple, the altar and those who worship there. Amplified says it this way; *"A reed [as a measuring rod] was then given to me, [shaped] like a staff, and I was told: Rise up and measure the sanctuary of God and the altar [of incense], and [number] those who worship there."* The measuring rod indicates that something is about to be built. This is also indicated in Zechariah 4:9-10, *"The hands the Zerubbabel have laid the foundation of this temple; his hands shall also finish it. Then you will know that the Lord of hosts has sent Me to you. For who has despised the day of small things? For these seven rejoice to see the plumb line in the hand of Zerubbabel."* Ezekiel 40:3 also mentions a measuring rod: *"He took me there, and behold, there was a man whose appearance was like the appearance of bronze. He had a line of flax and a measuring rod in his hand."* Ezekiel was a prophet during the Jewish exile to Babylon and Zechariah was a prophet during the rebuilding of the temple after the exile. So we see in chapter 11 of Revelation that the measuring rod is a prophetic sign that something is about to be built. Then two prophets emerge in the streets of Jerusalem. This could be looked at as God's "last call." They are described as the two olive trees and lampstands that stand before God (Zechariah.4:11-14). They prophesy three and one-half years in the streets of Jerusalem. Question for those of you who have been to visit Jerusalem: "Would prophesying about Jesus on the streets of Jerusalem be possible in this present day without ending in a violent encounter?"

You will notice in Revelation 11:5 that they have been given power like Elijah had been given power when confronted by a captain with 50 men: *"He spoke to him: "Man of God, the king has said, 'Come down!' So Elijah answered and said to the captain of fifty, 'If I am a man of God, then let fire come down from heaven and consume you and your fifty men.' And fire came down from heaven and consumed him and his fifty"* (2 Kings 1:9-10). These two prophets also face extreme danger: *"If anyone wants to harm them, fire proceeds from their mouth and devours their enemies. And if anyone wants to harm them, he must be killed in this manner."* If Jerusalem is being trampled by the Gentiles (Muslim nations) and a third of mankind has just been killed, these two prophets need this power in order to just survive. They prophesy three-and-one-half years with this power! It also says in verse 6, *"These have power to shut heaven, so that no rain falls in the days of their prophecy; and they have power over waters to turn them to blood, and to strike the earth with all plagues, as often as they desire."* In other words they can do this whenever they want. God trusts them completely! After three-and-one-half years, they are confronted by a **beast**. (I'm sure he doesn't look like a beast, otherwise he couldn't deceive people like he does.) The Scripture says, *"When they finish their testimony, the **beast** that **ascends out of the bottomless pit** will make war against them, overcome them, and kill them."* (emphasis mine) I'm not sure what this will all look like, but these prophets are giving testimony of Jesus the Messiah! The beast that ascends out of the bottomless pit has the same description as the beast the harlot is sitting on in Revelation 17:8, *"The beast that you saw* (carrying the harlot) *was,* *and is not, and will **ascend out of the bottomless pit** and go to perdition."* (emphasis mine) I believe this beast is not like the first beast in Revelation 13:1, but is a false messiah or Christ as described in Revelation 13:11-14. The harlot of Revelation 17 and 18 (described in my book, *The Counterfeit Woman*) thinks she is the bride and is following a messiah. She's claiming his second coming, yet he is straight out of the pit of hell! This beast overcomes the two prophets, as described in chapter 11, and has them killed. Notice that their dead bodies are left to rot in the streets of Jerusalem for three-and-one-half days. All the while those who are of the world are partying and sending gifts to one another as if it were Christmas. The reason: the two prophets tormented them! The light of God's glory and the power of God's word through Christ in them tormented the people that were in Jerusalem. These people were very relieved when these two prophets had been killed. Today, we see celebration in the nations surrounding Israel whenever a Jew is murdered. Is this just the beginning of the end of days? What is described in Revelation 11:11-12 reminds me of an old Christian friend of mine. He so wanted to be raptured while he was sharing Jesus with sinners out on the streets. He wanted this to happen right before their very eyes. This Scripture says it happened just this way; *"Now after the three-and-a-half days the breath of life from God entered them, and they stood on their feet, and great fear fell on those who saw them. And they heard a loud voice from heaven saying to them, 'Come up here.' And they ascended to heaven in a cloud, and their enemies saw them."* My friend went to be with Jesus several years ago without seeing this happen. This one's for you, Dave!

CHAPTER 10

THE MYSTERY OF GOD

"In the days of the sounding of the seventh angel, when he is about to sound, the mystery of God would be finished, as He declared to His servants the prophets." Revelation 10:7

What is the mystery of God that is talked about here? It says the mystery would be finished at and during the days of the trumpet sound of the seventh angel. In between this statement in Revelation 10:7 that the angel who is standing on the sea and earth just proclaimed, and the seventh trumpet being sounded in Revelation 11:15, we witness two prophets in Jerusalem giving testimony of Jesus for three-and-one-half years. To repeat: They are under divine protection. They finish their testimony and are killed by the beast. These two prophets were overcome and killed, yet after three days the breath of God entered them. Their very resurrection and ascension to heaven was witnessed by all in Jerusalem. What happens next in Revelation 11:13 seems to be an exclamation point of this event! *"In the same hour there was a great earthquake, and a tenth of the city fell. In the earthquake, seven thousand people were killed, and the rest were afraid and gave glory to the God of heaven."* I believe these events are the catalyst that set in motion the salvation of the Jews. This is a great part of the mystery that is spoken of. The testimony and prophecy that these two prophets gave for three-and-one-half years found hearts that had good soil which produced one hundred fold! As we look into chapter 12 we see a great sign: The Jews being saved and God using them to defeat the enemy of all mankind. We also see that the second woe has been completed and the third woe is now coming quickly. There is quite a lot to wrap your head around from now on! We must remember this is a revelation and not just information. Revelations can't be figured out in our minds. They must be illuminated in our hearts and minds. The whole of Scripture must be taken into account in order to see God's very heart in these things; otherwise we will only have a small part of the picture which will always leave us confused or deceived.

A WOMAN?
"Now a great sign appeared in heaven: A woman."
Revelation 12:1

Who was this woman? Her description has significant meaning. Why is she described as crying out in labor to give birth? Isaiah describes a woman in his book; chapter 26:16-18, *"Lord, in trouble they have visited You, they poured out a prayer when Your chastening was upon them. As a woman with child is in pain and cries out in her pangs, when she draws near the time of her delivery, so have we been in Your sight, O Lord. We have been with child, we have been in pain; we have, as it were, brought forth wind."* Both of these women described in Isaiah and Revelation are in labor pains. Both are crying out in their pain to give birth! To shed more light on this we must look to Isaiah: *"Behold, the virgin shall conceive and bear a Son, and shall call His name Immanuel."* (7:14) *and* *"For unto us a Child is born, unto us a Son is given; and the government will be upon His shoulder. And His name will be called Wonderful, Counselor, Mighty God, Everlasting Father, Prince of Peace."* (9:6)

Israel is described as a woman in labor and in pain to give birth. Isaiah says that in her pain she has only brought forth wind and that's all. God gives Israel the promise of a Messiah right in the midst of her backsliding and rebellion. His chastening and judgment is upon her which brings pain, but she does not change. God still promises His Son to them even in the midst of her backslidings. Notice what Isaiah proclaims about her in Isaiah 66:7-8, *"Before she was in labor, she gave birth; before her pain came, she delivered a male child. Who has heard such a thing? Who has seen such things?"* God is saying through Isaiah that Israel gave birth to Jesus long before she was actually in labor pains! Jesus is the child that she has given birth to, just as it says in Revelation 12:5, *"She bore a male Child who was to rule all nations with a rod of iron. And her Child was caught up to God and His throne."* If she was given the Messiah why is she described as only bringing forth wind? It began in Isaiah 6 when God told Isaiah to tell the people, *"Keep on hearing, but do not understand; keep on seeing, but do not perceive. Make the heart of this people dull, and their ears heavy, and shut their eyes; lest they see with their eyes, and hear with their ears, and understand with their heart, and return and be healed."* Jesus quoted this Scripture when His disciples came and asked Him why He always speaks to the people (the Jews) in parables. He answered them starting with these words: *"Because it has been given to you to know the mysteries of the kingdom of heaven, but to them it has not been given. Therefore I speak to them in parables."* (Matthew 13:11,13) The first time this passage was opened up to me, I saw Jesus as hiding the kingdom of God from the Jews. It was almost as if He didn't want anyone to have the revelation that He was the Messiah. Could it be that God had us Gentiles on His heart and didn't want us left out of His kingdom? He hardened Israel's heart so we could be brought in. Then in the fullness of time, when the fullness of the Gentiles has come in, He again brings Israel to the place of birth pangs as mentioned in Revelation 12:1,2 and 5; *"Now a great sign appeared in heaven; a woman clothed with the sun, with the moon under her feet, and on her head a garland of twelve stars. Then being with child, she cried out in labor and in pain to give birth."* -- *"She bore a male Child who was to rule all nations with a rod of iron. And her Child was caught up to God and His throne."* Micah also says in his book, *"He shall give them* (Zion) *up, Until the time that she who is in labor has given birth."* (5:3) I ask you, "Have we almost reached this point in history?" Are we seeing the beginning stages of the woman in labor? This woman is to change the destiny of the world and radically alter the influence that Satan has had on the people of God! After these two signs are described, we see war breaking out in heaven. Michael and his angels are warring with Satan and his angels. Daniel was also given prophetic revelation on this very thing: *"At that time Michael shall stand up, The great prince who stands watch over the sons of your people* (Israel)*; and there shall be a time of trouble, such as never was since there was a nation, even to that time. And at that time your people shall be delivered, every one who is found written in the book."* (Daniel 12:1) Michael is the prince of Israel and as we see in Revelation 12, he is warring against Satan. Notice what happens after this in Revelation 12:7-9, *"The dragon and his angels fought, but they did not prevail, nor was a place found for them in heaven any longer. So the great dragon was **cast out**, that serpent of old, called the Devil and Satan, who deceives the whole world; **he was cast to the earth**, and his angels were cast out with him."* (emphasis mine) I ask you, HAS THIS HAPPENED YET? Remember what Revelation 1:1 says, *"God gave Him* (Jesus, a revelation of Himself) *to show His servants -- things which must shortly take place."* In other words these things have not happened yet! I haven't seen two prophets in the streets of Jerusalem killing their enemies with fire from their mouths and then being resurrected and caught up to heaven! I haven't seen an earthquake destroying a tenth of Jerusalem and seven thousand people killed because of it! Even further; I haven't seen stinging bugs tormenting man for 5 months (first woe). I haven't seen a third of mankind killed (second woe). However, I don't think we are very far away from these things happening! If you don't know Jesus, talk to Him and ask Him to forgive you, wash you, and make you His own. He does love you!

THE WOMAN / OUR BRETHREN = THEY

As we see Satan cast out of heaven there is a loud voice that comes from heaven saying, *"Now salvation, and strength, and the kingdom of our God, and the power of His Christ have come, for the accuser of **our brethren**, who accused them before our God day and*

107

night, has been cast down" (12:10 - emphasis mine). This same loud voice also speaks the following words; *"And **they** overcame him by the blood of the Lamb and by the word of **their** testimony, and **they** did not love **their** lives to the death."* (12:11 - emphasis mine) The accused brethren mentioned are also those who overcame the Devil. The woman who gave birth is the same woman who fled into the wilderness from Satan where she is fed for three-and-one-half years (12:6). If this great sign started with a woman in labor and ended with a woman fleeing into the wilderness, then she is described as "our brethren", and would be referred to as "they" in Revelation 12:11 *"They overcame him"*. We, as Gentile believers, have been given a promise along side the Jewish believers. It's written to a Gentile church: *"He who overcomes, and keeps My works until the end, to him I will give power over the nations."* (Revelation 2:26) Then again in Revelation 3:21 *"To him who overcomes I will grant to sit with Me on My throne, as I also overcame and sat down with My Father on His throne."* As we have seen, the woman is Israel. Israel is in labor and finally gives birth. Jesus becomes their Messiah! Paul mentions this in Romans 11:25-26, *"Blindness has happened to Israel until the fullness of the Gentiles . . . And so all Israel will be saved."* The next verse in Revelation 12:12 is, in my estimation, one of the most misquoted verses in the Bible. I have heard this verse in many sermons by many preachers that talk as if this has already happened. They say, *"The devil has great wrath, because he knows that he has a short time!"* In order to see the truth in this we must back up and consider what just happened. Satan was cast out of heaven and was cast to the earth because they (Israel) overcame him. The loud voice which spoke from heaven is speaking again in verse 12 saying, *"Therefore rejoice, O heavens, and you who dwell in them!"* This was said because Satan had just been cast out of heaven! *"Woe to the inhabitants of the earth and the sea!"* This was said because Satan was being cast to the earth! He no longer has influence in the heavenlies. He will only be able to move and operate on the earth from this time on! *"Rejoice, O heavens and you who dwell in them!"* The "woe" spoken to the earth's inhabitants is because Satan has been cast there to live out the rest of his days (three-and-one-half years)! This makes me shutter because he will have total control over the earth for three-and-one-half years. Remember, Jesus warned in Matthew 24:22, *"Unless those days* *were shortened, no flesh would be saved; but for the elect's sake those days will be shortened."* I would think if there was a rapture before this happened "the elect" would not be spoken of here. If you have a hard time receiving these things, please study them for yourself. God would be most willing to reveal His mysteries.

A DRAGON---FIERY RED

"And another sign appeared in heaven: behold, a great fiery red dragon having seven heads and ten horns."
Revelation 12:3

This dragon spoken of is Satan: *"So the great dragon was cast out, that serpent of old, called the Devil and Satan."* (Revelation 12:9) He is described as the "serpent of old" from the garden of Eden. The originator of sin, death, and destruction in the earth. I often ask myself, "When did he change from a serpent into a dragon?" His very description is exactly the same as the description of the beast in Revelation 13:1, 17:3, and Daniel 7:7. He is described as having seven heads and ten horns. The beast and Satan have exactly the same description. Jesus speaks of Daniel's beast in Matthew 24:15, *"Therefore when you see the **abomination of desolation**, spoken of by Daniel the prophet."* In this, we see that Satan (posed as the abomination) is given all power and authority over the earth when he becomes "the abomination" who fills the desolation. It is at this time that Satan pours out all of his character and evil schemes upon mankind. His temptations and suggestions are not just in thought anymore, but he enforces his will with great ruthless authority. He's not in the heavens anymore. He is in full presence upon this earth and gives birth to his version of a messiah. Hear what is being said in Revelation 13:11-12, *"Then I saw another beast coming up out of the earth, and he had two horns like a lamb and spoke like a dragon. And he exercises all the authority of the first beast in his presence, and causes the earth and those who dwell in it to worship the first beast."* His desire is worship as it says in Revelation 13:4, *"So they worshipped the dragon who gave authority to the beast; and they worshipped the beast, saying, 'Who is like the beast? Who is able to make war with him?' "* I would have to say that this sounds like what we are seeing in and through radical Islam. They are ruthless in their pursuit of power and dominance over the earth. They hate Israel and accuse her continually. They have often talked of her destruction. They serve Allah who they proclaim as God, creator of all things. As they destroy and methodically conquer through fear and intimidation, people and even nations, there seems to be one cry that comes out of their mouth: "Allah Akbar" which means "God is greater" or "God is [the] greatest"[8] Wouldn't this be blasphemy? Claiming deity to one who kills and destroys? We also see that the dragon gave the beast his power, his throne, and great authority. Everything we will see in this beast is what Satan has given him. It says he was given a mouth speaking great things and blasphemies. If this beast were a man, he would already have a mouth and no need to be given one. We also see in chapter 13:12 that the man of sin (the second beast from the earth) *"exercises all the authority of the first beast in his presence."* (emphasis mine) Doesn't this sound unusual? The second beast is **in the presence of the first beast**! Another unusual statement is in 13:14, *"He deceives those who dwell on the earth by those signs which he was granted to do in the sight of the beast."* (emphasis mine) The first beast sounds like he is all seeing. This beast is given a mouth, is ever present, and is all seeing. Doesn't this sound like he would be spirit instead of flesh and blood? We must understand that Jesus performed miracles and cast out demons in the presence of the Father. Since the second beast exercises authority and performs great signs in the presence of the first beast, we would have to conclude that the first beast is a manifestation of Satan in all his character.

DEADLY HEAD WOUND

The beast is described as having a deadly wound on his head. In chapter 13 we see the phrase, *"his deadly wound was healed,"* appears twice in this chapter. Then the phrase *"the beast who was wounded by the sword and lived"* appears. We conclude that this is a man with a wound on his head and he lived through it. I completely disagree with this conclusion and here's why. Throughout the prophets we see the sword being spoken of in regard to the destruction of human life. Isaiah 1:20 says if you are not willing to be obedient to the Lord (but refuse and rebel), you will be devoured

---

[8] https://en.wikipedia.org/wiki/Takbir

by the sword. Assyria and Babylon came and fulfilled this. Other verses of Scripture which refer to the sword devouring are Isaiah 34:5-6, 66:16; Jeremiah 12:12, 46:10, 47:6, 50:35-37. Ezekiel chapter 21 and 33:1-11 describe the sword in its destruction. Whenever Scripture expounds on the use of the sword, it always refers to ending human life and purging evil. Throughout history we have seen the rise and fall of many empires and kings. All these have fallen because of war and destruction which the Scripture refers to as "the sword." The beast of Revelation 13 has seven heads of which one has a deadly wound which was healed. In verse 14, we see the beast himself was wounded by the sword and lived. If the beast is "spirit," then we can only conclude that he is wounded because the sword comes against his followers. He is wounded from dominating the earth because his followers are destroyed. Isn't this what we see happening today with Islamic extremists? We are at war with terrorism and seek to wipe out these terrorist groups because they threaten the very existence of Israel and the whole western world, including America. Israel, and the whole western world, have declared war on terror and seek to control it. But the Scripture says "he is wounded by the sword and lived"! Islam has been growing into an extremely large following up to this day. At present, they seek to dominate and fly their flags over much of the world. I perceive that even though we wound them severely, they will rebound aggressively and continue in their pursuit of world domination. This is a prophetic word given in the book of Revelation (chapter 17:12-13, 16-17) and must be fulfilled in order for all enemies to be made a footstool for the Lord!

HE WAS GRANTED

Within Revelation 13, we see something else that could be misunderstood. Along with this beast being given a mouth, it was also granted to him to make war with the saints and to overcome them (verse 7). Who granted this? This same thing appears in regard to the second beast. He was granted the ability to perform signs in order to deceive and he also was granted the power to give breath to the image of the first beast (verses 14 and 15).. Again, I must ask, "Who granted these things?" Jesus says in Matthew 24:24, *"False Christ's and false prophets will rise and show great signs and*

111

wonders **to deceive, if possible, even the elect.** *"* (emphasis mine) Jesus warned us of false Christ's and prophets in the last days, but what we are seeing in these beasts is the granting of great signs to deceive. What I am about to present must not be misunderstood, because God is a jealous God and extremely desires His people to follow Him without compromise. This Scripture is in the Bible and must be discerned correctly. *"If a prophet arises among you, or a dreamer of dreams, and gives you a sign or a wonder, and the sign or the wonder he foretells to you comes to pass, and if he says, Let us go after other gods---gods you have not known---and let us serve them, you shall not listen to the words of that prophet or to that dreamer of dreams.* **For the Lord your God is testing you** *to know whether you love the Lord your God with all your [mind and] heart and with your entire being."* (Deuteronomy 13:1-3 - AMP - emphasis mine) We can see that God does test His people to see what's in their heart. Look at the case of Job: Satan accused Job saying that he was not sincere in his love for God, but only served Him because of God's blessings. Satan said to God, *"Now, stretch out Your hand and touch all that he has, and he will surely curse You to Your face! And the Lord said to Satan, 'Behold, all that he has is in your power; only do not lay a hand on his person.' "* (Job 1:11-12) God granted this permission to Satan. You might say right here that Satan had the right to do this because of original sin and that Adam gave all he had to Satan when he fell into sin. True. But God Himself did test Job as we see in the next verses. *"Then the Lord said to Satan, 'Have you considered My servant Job, that there is none like him on the earth, a blameless and upright man, one who fears God and shuns evil? And still he holds fast to his integrity,* **although you incited Me against him**, *to destroy him without cause.' So Satan answered the Lord and said, 'Skin for skin! Yes, all that a man has he will give for his life. But stretch out Your hand now, and touch his bone and his flesh, and he will surely curse You to Your face!' And the Lord said to Satan,* **'Behold, he is in your hand**, *but spare his life.' "* (Job 2:3-6 - emphasis mine) Job's testing was granted to Satan by God. The granting to these beasts in Revelation 13 is also granted by God. The hearts and minds of all mankind will be tested in these days. What will come forth from these tests will look like the people in Revelation 7:9-17 and 14:1-5. *"These* (like the first fruits) *are the ones who come out of the great tribulation and washed their robes and made them white in the blood* *of the Lamb!"* (7:14) Jesus also grants something, but it's to the overcomer: *"To him who overcomes I will grant to sit with Me on My throne, as I also overcame and sat down with My Father on His throne"* (Revelation 3:21) How can someone grant something if they don't have the authority and power to do so?

666

"He causes all, both small and great, rich and poor, free and slave, to receive a mark on their right hand or on their foreheads"
Revelation 13:16.

Receiving a mark on the hand and forehead was originally God's idea. Exodus 13 makes this clear. The celebration of the Passover and the sacrificing of every first born male was to be a reminder of God's deliverance from Egypt. The Lord said concerning these things: *"It shall be as a sign to you on your **hand** and as a memorial **between your eyes**, that the Lord's law may be in your mouth; for with a strong hand the Lord has brought you out of Egypt."* (Exodus 13:9 - emphasis mine) Satan is a counterfeiter of the things of God. The mark on the right hand and forehead was not Satan's idea. When our right hand and forehead are in line with God, then He can direct our entire life. A chip implanted under our skin is not the mark of the beast and is not going to direct our lives. The receiving of the mark of the beast is directly in line with worshipping the beast. Scripture says *"he causes as many as would not worship the image of the beast to be killed. He causes all . . . to receive a mark."* This mark is clearly seen on those who bow down to Allah. It's a mark that is made on the forehead when Muslims bow down to pray to Allah and touch their foreheads on the ground. If you go to one of these web sights you will understand.[9] When it says that no one will buy or sell except the one who has the mark, the name, or the number of the name of the beast it means all will bow and worship this "beast." I believe life on this earth as we know it will cease, since a third of mankind will be killed in the sixth trumpet

---

[9] www.sunniforum.com/forum/archive/index.php/t-88986.html
http://islam.about.com/od/quran/a/ayats-sujood.htm

judgment. This will be a catastrophic event that will make resources of food and clothing a rare commodity.

So what's in a name? We see in John 3:18 that we must believe **in the name** of the only begotten Son of God. Jesus speaking to the Jews in John 5:43 said, *"I have come in My Father's name, and you do not receive Me; if another comes in his own name, him you will receive."* (emphasis mine) No one is allowed to buy or even sell anything unless they have the mark or the name of the beast. If his name is Allah and you believe in and worship him, then you have his name. Jesus said an amazing thing concerning Satan when addressing Peter after Peter had rebuked Him for saying He was going to be killed. *"Get behind Me, Satan! You are an offense to Me, for you are not mindful of the things of God, **but the things of men.**"* (Matthew 16:23 - emphasis mine) We see this throughout all of Scripture. Men stopped worshipping God and made idols for themselves in their own likeness. This beast and image is the product of Satan's mindfulness of the things of men. This is not just an idol who cannot see or hear, but a spiritual force producing miraculous signs and wonders to deceive all mankind. Philippians 2:9 says *"God also has highly exalted Him* (Jesus) *and given Him the name, which is above every name."* Jesus spoke to John in the Revelation saying, *"I am the Alpha and the Omega, the First and the Last."* Jesus has no number attached to His name since His name covers everything beginning to end; from the highest highs to the lowest lows, even to the farthest reaches of the universe. His name has no end! The beast on the other hand has a number attached to his name and even worse *"it is the number of a man."* [666] (Revelation 13:8)

ISLAM'S MESSIAH

The worship of Allah is methodically lived out on a daily basis. I do not know all the inner workings of prayer within Islam, but I see millions of Muslims falling on their faces simultaneously as they pray and worship Allah. They await a messiah just as Christian's await a return of The Messiah. They call this messiah the

Mahdi or the twelfth Imam[10]. This Mahdi is the beast with two horns like a lamb, speaking like a dragon. He will cause all to worship the first beast. Notice it says that he will exercise all the authority of the first beast in his presence. The Mahdi is a man and the first beast is a spirit or god (Allah). They also proclaim that God has no son. A friend of mine who has gone to Israel and visited the temple mount where the dome of the rock now stands has seen what is written on the outside of the mosque. In several places it says, "God has no son".[11] So the Mahdi would not be considered a son, but a flesh and blood manifestation of Allah. We know that God does have a Son and that He is sitting at the right hand of God waiting for His enemies to be made His footstool. He not only has One Son, but He has many sons and daughters. Those who have been born again and follow Jesus closely are His sons and daughters. Many claim to be His sons, but are not walking as a son. The love of the world and the love of the flesh dominate in their lives. The word plainly states that if we love the world, we are enemies of God, *"Whoever therefore wants to be a friend of the world makes himself an enemy of God."* (James 4:4) As we see the book of Revelation unfold before our very eyes, we must consider that Jesus is coming very soon! If we are like the five foolish virgins who did not carry extra oil to burn in their lamps, we will hear the words, "I don't know you" when we knock on the door that has just been closed. This is a fearful thing! I would not want Jesus to look me in the eyes and say this to me! It would mean instant separation! This brings to mind the movie *It's A Wonderful Life*. The angel Clarence alters George Baily's life for a moment as if he had never been born. When he sees his wife Mary, she looks into his eyes and does not recognize him because he had not been born! The loving relationship that he once had with her did not exist, even though he thought it did. She did not know him! When I stand before Jesus I want Him to look at me as a lover who has endeavored to walk with Him and know Him. I want Him to see the marks of God in my life. The marks of blessing and the marks of discipline and even judgment. "Judge me now so I won't be judged when I stand before You!

---

[10] https://en.wikipedia.org/wiki/Mahdi
[11] http://tribulationproject.com/archives/355

TEN KINGS WITH NO KINGDOM

As we look at the dragon's endeavors to persecute the woman, we see all his efforts fail. We must remember that all these things are happening after a third of mankind has been killed on the earth. Israel is still around and has not been destroyed by the Iranian regime as they have threatened to do. As the dragon sees himself cast to the earth and his efforts to derail the woman fail, he is enraged in frustration as we see in Revelation 12:17, *"And the dragon was enraged with the woman, and he went to make war with the rest of her offspring, who keep the commandments of God and have the testimony of Jesus Christ."* That would be us. Notice what happens after *"he went to make war with the rest of her offspring."* John says, *"Then I stood on the sand of the sea. And I saw a beast rising up out of the sea . . ."* I believe this is Allah, Islam's god. Notice this beast has ten horns. I believe these ten horns are radical terrorist extremist groups. There is a website listing organizations that are designated as terrorist groups. This website has a list of 160 groups that would be designated by many nations of the world. Most of these are not in the news today. There are only a handful that make the news on a daily basis. I will list them as I have seen them: Al Queda, Al Shabaab, Ansar al-Sharia, Boko Haram, Hamas, Hezbollah, Islamic Jihad, Taliban, Muslim Brotherhood, and ISIS (or Islamic State). I see ten that are prominently broadcasted in the news. The number 10 is not a hard number, but a number that fluctuates. A detailed description of these ten horns is given in Revelation 17:12-14, 16-17. As I list these Scriptures, you will notice a resemblance to the groups mentioned.

- *"The ten horns which you saw are ten kings who have received no kingdom as yet, but they receive authority for one hour as kings with the beast."* Each one of these groups has a leader. They are referred to as kings with no kingdom. These would be considered rogue kings. Their mandate is for Allah to have supreme authority over the earth. When the beast comes into power they will rule with him, but only for a short period of time. This would be likened unto the "little book" that the angel had open in his hand or the three-and-one-half year period.

- *"These are of one mind, and they will give their power and authority to the beast."* They are not out to become rulers in this earth, but to see Allah's mandate for the earth come to pass. They all have the same agenda in mind: The worship of Allah and the dominance of his law throughout the earth (Sharia law).

- *"These will make war with the Lamb, and the Lamb will overcome them, for He is Lord of lords and King of kings; and those who are with Him are chosen and faithful."* Every one of these groups would punish someone who claims to be a follower of Jesus. At present, Christians are being methodically sought out and killed by these groups. Through terror they are reigning as lords and kings and again, are only wanting the worship of Allah throughout the earth. Jesus is Lord of all lords and King of all kings. We who are with Him (in His persecutions and sufferings) are chosen and faithful.

- *"The **ten horns** which you saw on the beast, these will hate the harlot, make her desolate and naked, eat her flesh and burn her with fire. **For God has put it into their hearts to fulfill His purpose**, to be of one mind, and to give their kingdom to the beast, until the words of God are fulfilled."* (emphasis mine) These kings are observing a people presently that claim to walk with God, but in reality they are a harlot as is specifically described in Ezekiel 16. A people that claim God's name, but live like the world. Throughout Scripture we see this very thing. Most all of the kings of Israel were wicked and all Israel followed suit. Today we see this in many churches and in many Christians who walk half-hearted with Jesus. These ten kings call these half-hearted believers infidels. The definition of infidel is unfaithful, a disbeliever in something specified or understood. In other words it is understood what Jesus says, yet what He says is not followed or obeyed. Claiming His favor and blessing is priority, but living like He did is not desired. Jesus said, *"If you love Me, keep My commandments."* There is much more I could expound on concerning the harlot, but won't at this

time. Concerning the ten kings; God has put it in **their** hearts to fulfill His purpose. I know this is confusing to some, yet we must look at the scriptural pattern set in the Old Testament. In the book of Jeremiah, we see the plan of God to use Babylon to discipline Israel for 70 years. If you read through this book, you will see God's heart in this. He first spoke about this happening in Deuteronomy 28:15,32,48-50: *"But it shall come to pass, if you do not obey the voice of the Lord your God, to observe carefully all His commandments and His statutes which I command you today, that all these curses will come upon you and overtake you."*
"Your sons and your daughters shall be given to another people . . . "
"You shall serve your enemies, whom the Lord will send against you . . . The Lord will bring a nation against you from afar, from the end of the earth . . . a nation of fierce countenance, which does not respect the elderly nor show favor to the young."
These things did come to pass. Because of Israel not obeying the Lord's voice, He says through Jeremiah in chapter 18:11, *"Behold, I am fashioning a disaster and devising a plan against you. Return now every one from his evil way."* And then it happened. Babylon came and set up their rule in Israel. Notice what the captain of Babylon's guard says to Jeremiah after they conquered Jerusalem; *"The Lord your God has pronounced this doom on this place. Now the Lord has brought it, and has done just as He said. Because you people have sinned against the Lord, and not obeyed His voice, therefore this thing has come upon you."* Who told Babylon, an ungodly nation, that they would be used to bring doom upon Israel because they had sinned and not obeyed Gods voice? God did. So we can also see this very thing happening in the last days with these ten kings as well. This should cause us to stand up and take notice. Are we any different than Israel? Why would God ignore our sin and disobedience to His voice when He held Israel accountable. This nation was once known as a Christian nation, but now is known by Muslim nations as a nation of infidels.

118

We must understand that what is seen by John in regard to the beasts and their followers is actually the seventh trumpet judgment or the third woe mentioned in Revelation 11:14, *"Behold the third woe is coming quickly."* The third woe has to do with the beast ruling in Israel and the implementation of his kingdom through him receiving worship as God. To complicate the understanding of this vision even more, we must understand that the seventh trumpet judgment (third woe) is part of the breaking of the seventh seal. The beast and his kingdom must be dealt with before the scroll is opened. Notice Revelation 8:1-2, *"When He opened the **seventh seal**, there was silence in heaven for about half an hour. And I saw the **seven angels** who stand before God, and **to them were given seven trumpets.**"* (emphasis mine) We have understood that the seals are to be broken off of the scroll in order for it to be read and released. Within these chapters 11-13, what is happening in Israel; the two prophets prophesying in Jerusalem for three-and-one-half years (chapter 11), the salvation of the Jews and they being fed in the wilderness for three-and-one-half years (chapter 12), and the beast having dominance over the earth for three-and-one-half years (chapter 13), has to be understood as part of the seventh seal being broken off of the scroll. The seals are hindering God's glorious plan from coming into fruition. Remember the angel proclaiming in chapter 10:5-7 that the mystery of God would be finished **in the days** of the trumpet sounding **of the seventh angel**. At this sounding the last seal will be broken off of the scroll.

THE SCROLL IS OPENED
"Then I looked, and behold, a Lamb standing on Mount Zion, and with Him 144,000, having His Father's name written on their foreheads" Revelation 14:1.

We just left chapter 13 with those who took the mark of the beast on their hand or *forehead* in order to do business on the earth. They sold out to the beast. Then we see the firstfruits of God and the Lamb: 144,000 having their Father's name written on their *foreheads*. The description of these is in direct contrast with the wicked observed in Revelation 9:20-21 which says, *Mankind **did not repent** of the worship of demons, and idols of gold, silver, brass, stone, and wood. . . and **they did not repent** of their murders or their* sorceries, or their sexual immorality or their thefts." (emphasis mine) The 144,000 are described in this way: *"They sang as it were a new song before the throne, before the four living creatures, and the elders; and no one could learn that song except the 144,000 who were redeemed from the earth."* I would interpret a new song as something that has never been sung before. Within the description of these mentioned, we see the contents of this new song. *"These are the ones who **were not defiled with women**, for they are virgins.* (Considering the days we presently live in, this in itself would be a new song!) *These are the ones who **follow the Lamb wherever He goes**. These were redeemed from among men, being firstfruits to God and to the Lamb. And **in their mouth was found no deceit**, for they are **without fault** before the throne of God"* (*Revelation 14:3-5 - emphasis mine*). When I look around at this world, I'm not sure I see anyone that would be close to this description. They chose to live this way and God honored them. This contrast between those who did not repent and those who follow the Lamb wherever He goes reminds me of a couple verses. The first is in Revelation 22:11, *"He who is unjust, let him be unjust still; he who is filthy, let him be filthy still; he who is righteous, let him be righteous still, he who is holy, let him be holy still."* When you see Jesus coming in the clouds, it will be very hard to realize true repentance at that moment and not try and fake it. God will know if we have truth in our hearts or if we are trying to just put on obedience. Daniel puts it this way: *"And he [the angel] said, 'Go your way, Daniel, for the words are shut up and sealed till **the time of the end**. Many shall purify themselves and make themselves white and be tried, smelted, and refined, but the wicked shall do wickedly. And none of the wicked shall understand."* (*Daniel 12:11 - AMP - emphasis mine*) As it says in Revelation 7:14, *"They* (God's elect) *washed their robes and made them white in the blood of the Lamb."* Please forgive me for being so blunt, but I must state: If you find it hard to understand what is happening in these last days, and Daniel says the wicked will not understand, then it would stand to reason that maybe there is a compartmentalized wickedness that dominates the heart. Seeing the closeness of Jesus' return, I would seek the Lord most earnestly in Scripture and prayer in order to see clearly and maintain a pure and holy heart before God. I John 3:2-3 clarifies this: *"We know that when He is revealed, we shall be like Him, for we shall see Him as*

He is. And everyone who has this hope in Him purifies himself, just as He is pure." Purity, as Jesus is pure, comes from having our hope in Him; that when He comes back, we will be just like Him in His glorified, eternal state. Paul says, *"Now we see in a mirror dimly, but then face to face."* We have our hope in this face to face encounter that will make us forever like Him. This hope must cause in us the desire for purity. Jesus puts it this way, *"Blessed are the pure in heart, for they shall see God."* (Matthew 5:8) Wouldn't it stand to reason that if we are not pure in heart, we will not see God (His face shining on us?)

The attitude of the wicked servant who thought his Master was delaying His coming was not looked at with joy by the Master. The wicked servant had let down his guard and began to eat and drink with drunkards (those who are drunk on earthly things). He was no longer in the place of holiness and readiness. He was seeing how close he could get to the fire and not be burned. It says when the Master returns on a day when he is not looking for Him, and finds him in this condition *"He will cut him in two and appoint him his portion with the hypocrites. There shall be weeping and gnashing of teeth."* (Matthew 24:51) This does not sound like a good outcome for one who had been called "a servant."

CHAPTER **11**

THE CONCEPTION AND PROGRESSION OF IDOL WORSHIP

"In the beginning God created the heavens and the earth. The earth was without form, and void; and darkness was on the face of the deep. And the Spirit of God was hovering over the face of the waters. Then God said, 'LET THERE BE LIGHT', and there was light. And God saw the light, that it was good; **and God divided the light from the darkness**. *God called the light Day, and the darkness He called Night."* (Genesis 1:1-5 - emphasis mine)

Why was there darkness on the face of the deep in the beginning before man was created and put into the garden of Eden, which was paradise without the touch of death upon it? In the whole of Scripture, darkness was something that was to be avoided at all costs. Why did God divide the light from the darkness if darkness was part of His creation? Have you ever asked God these questions?

John asked these questions and then addressed them in his books. He writes: *"In the beginning was the Word, and the Word was with God, and the Word was God. He was in the beginning with God. All things were made through Him, and without Him nothing was made that was made. In Him was life, and the life was the light of men. And the light shines in the **darkness**, and the **darkness** did not comprehend it."* (John 1:1-4 - emphasis mine)

John is proclaiming that Jesus was the Word and the Light that came into the world. We know this because when Jesus came into our lives, He radically transformed us within. He pulled us out of the darkness and established us in His kingdom of light. We are forever thankful for this! God is establishing light in His people through Jesus and as we respond to this light (His Word), we become more like Him. I love it!

DARKNESS ON THE FACE

When I look at the Scripture in Genesis 1, I can't help but ask why there was darkness in the beginning. I turn to 1 John 1:1-5 which says, *"That which was from the beginning, which we have heard, which we have seen with our eyes . . . This is the message which we have heard from Him and declare to you, THAT GOD IS LIGHT AND **IN HIM IS NO DARKNESS** AT ALL."* (emphasis mine) This compels me to ask again: "If God is light and there is no darkness in Him at all, why was there darkness on the face of the deep in the beginning?" He named the darkness night, and thus since the beginning and throughout Scripture, this darkness (night) has prevailed. We see in Revelation 21:25 and 22:5 that in the new Jerusalem, which is in the new heaven and earth, that *"There shall be no night there."* Since night represents darkness, I take it to mean there will be no darkness there. The darkness that was on the face of the deep has been eliminated! As we look into these things, I must say that I can't be dogmatic about what I present because Scripture isn't really clear on this subject. You must study for yourself.

Seeing darkness in the beginning would mean that darkness was around as Adam met with God in the garden. Many say they would like life to be as it was back in the garden. My response is "no way," because there was darkness and also the tree of knowledge of good and evil. Evil existed in the garden in this tree. I believe when the serpent spoke to Eve, that evil or darkness was manifested. It came out of hiding, so to speak. The creation of man and what God had instilled within man is what brought it out of hiding. *"The serpent was more cunning than any beast of the field which the Lord God had made. And **he said** . . . "* (Genesis 3:1 - emphasis mine) It was his very **speaking** that brought him out in the open, and the creation of man is what brought him out. God **spoke** light into darkness and then separated them. The serpent **spoke** darkness, because he was that darkness on the face of the deep. After the temptation and the fall, we hear the sound of God walking in the garden calling out to Adam and Eve. They were afraid and hid because they were naked. God asked Adam, *"Who told you that you were naked? Have you eaten from the tree of which I commanded you that you should not eat?"* It wasn't that God was clueless of this event, but He had to ask Adam so that Adam would become aware of the magnitude of what he had done. We know that Adam blamed Eve and that Eve blamed the serpent, but notice God's response to each one. To Adam He asked the question *"Who told you that you were naked?"* To Eve He asked the question *"What is this you have done?"* You will notice that God did not ask the serpent a question, but immediately pronounced judgment; *"Because you have done this, you are cursed above all [domestic] animals and above every [wild] living thing of the field; upon your belly you shall go, and you shall eat dust [and what it contains] all the days of your life."* (Genesis 3:14 - AMP) Satan speaking darkness made him manifest. The creation of man is how God will deal and eventually eradicate Satan and darkness forever. In the beginning, God gave man dominion over all. Hebrews 2:8 confirms this again: *"You have put **all** things in subjection under his* (man's) *feet. For in that He put **all** in subjection under him. He left nothing that is not put under him."* (emphasis mine) Many would ask why God didn't just throw Satan in the lake of fire at the very beginning. I don't know! We will find out in eternity. What we do know, and only find in Scripture, is that we must grow in grace and the knowledge of our Lord and Savior Jesus Christ. (2Peter 3:18) How much knowledge of Jesus beyond His death and resurrection do you possess? He is found in Scripture from Genesis to Revelation! Have you searched for these or are you satisfied with just a ticket to heaven and fire insurance from hell? Also, just attending church on Sunday will only give you someone's day-old manna. Asking God to give us this day our daily bread means we need daily to feed on His word.

DARKNESS INCREASES

In Genesis 6, we see that darkness (wickedness) had increased at a very rapid rate. It came to the point that God observed that no man would walk in what He had created him to be except one: Noah. *"Noah found grace in the eyes of the Lord."* (Genesis 6:8) So a complete destruction of man came by way of a flood and man was wiped out except for eight people. You will notice that all the animals came to Noah. He had dominion over them as God had proclaimed when He created man. Darkness was still in the earth even after man was destroyed. We see this happen almost immediately after the flood. One of Noah's own sons gave into darkness and saw his father's nakedness and then went out and told his brothers. I believe Ham's son, Canaan, was with him and saw it also. The Scripture says, *"Ham, the father of Canaan, saw the nakedness of his father."* What was the nakedness of Noah? Was Noah in a drunken stupor lying naked on the floor of his tent? Leviticus 18:8 says *"The nakedness of your father's wife you shall not uncover; it is your father's nakedness."* According to this verse Ham could have seen both Noah and his wife naked and told his brothers about it. It indicates twice that Ham was the father of Canaan, so Canaan must have been with him. The death of all mankind in the flood, because of their wickedness, was still fresh in Noah's mind. What Ham had done was a major infraction, not only against himself, but against his own son. The effects of Ham's decision on Canaan were irreversible. Noah didn't just randomly curse his grandson because of Ham's actions. Ham's actions brought the curse upon Canaan. Wickedness is passed on through generations. Only Jesus can break this curse so that our sons and daughters can be delivered.

After many years had transpired, God told Joshua and Israel to completely destroy the inhabitants of the land of Canaan because of the evil wickedness and darkness that inhabited this land. It was that the people of Canaan had gods other than the God of creation. Israel was commanded to destroy all of Canaan's inhabitants along with their gods which they had created. When Israel came to the place where they invaded Canaan, they did not do what God had commanded them to do. They did not utterly destroy all of Canaan's inhabitants, so Canaan's gods became a snare to Israel. God had covenanted and married Himself to Israel. We see this in Isaiah 62:4-5 (AMP) *"But you shall be called Hephzibah [My delight is in her], and your land be called Beulah [married]; for the Lord delights in you, and your land shall be married [owned and protected by the Lord] . . . and as the bridegroom rejoices over the bride, so shall your God rejoice over you."* God spoke this over Israel after they had invaded Canaan, but they didn't completely obey His word to destroy all idols. Israel was quickly ensnared in idol worship. Idols that God had commanded them to completely destroy. We see from this point on that idols were very much a part of Israel except in the days of David's reign as king. There were many times of reform where idols were destroyed, but they always fell back into this abomination. It was after David's reign that we begin to see the prophets Isaiah, Jeremiah, Ezekiel and many others come forth. God was speaking His message through them loud and clear and at the same time, He was preparing the manifestation of His Son on the earth. Jeremiah is a book that is almost one-hundred percent God's word or voice speaking to His people. The words *"The Lord said"* are recorded 400 times in this book. God expresses Himself to Israel through Jeremiah 10:2-5, *"Do not learn the way of the Gentiles . . . For one cuts a tree from the forest, the work of the hands of the workman, with the ax. They decorate it with silver and gold; they fasten it with nails and hammers so that it will not topple. They cannot speak; they must be carried, because they cannot go by themselves. Do not be afraid of them, for they cannot do evil, nor can they do any good."* The Lord tells Israel not to be afraid of these idols because they can't do evil. They are not alive! In Isaiah 44:14-17, the Lord endeavors to show Israel the foolishness of worshipping idols, *"He cuts down cedars for himself . . . Then it shall be for a man to burn, for he will take some of it and warm himself; Yes, he kindles it and bakes bread; indeed he makes a god and worships it; he makes it a carved image, and falls down to it. He burns half of it in the fire . . . and the rest of it he makes into a god . . . He falls down before it and worships it!"'* And we stand back, observe this behavior and say "How foolish! How could Israel have been so ignorant?" Having my own business, I have said this very thing regarding the contents in some of my client's homes that I go into; yet all the while endeavoring to make as much money as I could because I believed that God was prospering me. The truth be known; He was prospering me, but I was bowing down to the almighty dollar as if it would save me from sorrow. Greed is idolatry just as much as our possessions can be! Ezekiel 8:5-6 uncovers darkness and idol worship concerning Israel. *"He said to me, 'Son of man, lift your eyes now toward the north, and there, north of the altar gate, was this image of jealousy in the entrance. Furthermore He said to me, 'Son of man, do you see what they are doing, the great abominations that the house of Israel commits here, to make Me go far away from My sanctuary? Now turn again, you will see greater abominations.' "* This statement, *"you will see greater abominations"*, was spoken to Ezekiel three times. After each time, God showed him more of what Israel was doing in secret. God was revealing the secret sin of idol worship to the prophet. In Lamentations 2:14, we see the failure of the false prophet: *"Your prophets . . . they have not uncovered your iniquity . . . "* At the same time we see that the ministry of the prophet is to uncover man's iniquity; in private or in public. Idol worship is iniquity and must be uncovered or brought to light. Sometimes man does not see his iniquity until a man of God shows up.

Idol worship was a prominent sin in Israel throughout their days. Thanks to Jesus, we have been delivered from darkness and the worship of idols. Today we only see blatant worship of statues in some religions. These idols are still without speech or the power to deliver, except it seems that some are receiving words from these idols. The people who worship them say things like "Buddha has spoken to me!" Or "Mary has spoken to me!"[12] Do idols speak or is there a demonic force behind them speaking? Idol worship was a dominant part of life in Jesus' day. I John 5:21 says, *"Little children, keep yourselves from idols."* Paul also addresses this problem in

---

[12] http://www.medjugorjeusa.org/lourdes.htm

128

Colossians 3:5-6 (AMP), *"So kill (deaden, deprive of power) the evil desire lurking in your members [those animal impulses and all that is earthly in you that is employed in sin]: sexual vice, impurity, sensual appetites, unholy desires, and all greed and covetousness,* **for that is idolatry** *(the deifying of self and other created things instead of God)."* Today we see the deifying of self so blatantly before our very eyes. We also see the idolatry (deifying?) of things that man has in his possession: Houses, cars, Harleys, boats, places, movies, TV's, kid toys, adult toys, clothing, food, drugs (legal/illegal), alcohol, cigarettes, and the list goes on. Then we go on to created things like actors, musicians, models, comedians, football players, basketball players, golf players, tennis players, presidents, pets and even those who call themselves players. Again the list could go on and on. I hear people talk of these created things as if they are almost immortal. Just listen to a sport's announcer as he follows the game. Some people know more about team players than they know about God's plan of redemption. Some follow musicians and actors with a fervency unparalleled to anything else. I'm not talking about unholy, unbelieving, heathen cussers. These mentioned are adamantly and recklessly claiming to be a saved, holy follower of Jesus Christ! It's no wonder God is jealous. He sees His kids loving and following things of this world more aggressively than seeking His face in prayer and the Scriptures.

DARKNESS BECOMES AN IDOL

We have seen at the beginning of this chapter that darkness was on the face of the deep. God is in the deep which is His dwelling place; a place of the revelation of Himself. Satan is that darkness on the deep which perpetrates his own will and agenda. His desire is to be worshipped as we see in Isaiah 14:12-14, *"O Lucifer, son of the morning! You have said in your heart: 'I will ascend into heaven, I will exalt my throne above the stars of God; I will also sit on the mount of the congregation . . . I will ascend above the clouds, I will be like the Most High.'"* Satan's desire is to be like the Most High dwelling in the place of the deep and ruling over the creation of God. We can see this from the beginning of creation as he interacts with Adam and Eve. They gave their positions in God to Satan when they ate from the tree of knowledge of good and evil. In order to understand the prophecy of Revelation 13 regarding the beast rising up out of the sea, his image, and the beast coming out of the earth, we must refer to Genesis 1 and the beginning of creation.

Holy Spirit I ask You for clarity to be able to communicate this accurately.

In Genesis 1:2-10, we see the Spirit of God hovering over the face of the waters. This happened directly after darkness was seen on the face of the deep. God immediately spoke *"Let there be light"* and then He immediately divided the light from the darkness. Then in verses 6-7, God creates a firmament that divided the waters that were under the firmament from the waters that were above the firmament. For some reason, God saw that it was important to separate these waters. The waters under the firmament (heavens) were then gathered together into one place for which He called seas. Before we continue, it must be established that God had a purpose for dividing the waters. Ezekiel speaks of four living creatures that he had seen in a vision. He says when they went, he heard the sound of their wings, *"Like the noise of many waters, like the voice of the Almighty"* Ezekiel 1:24. Verses 25-26 says, *"A voice came from above the firmament . . . and above the firmament was a likeness of a throne."* Within these verses, we see that **God's voice** is like many **waters** and that His voice comes from **above** the firmament where His throne is established. We also see this in Ezekiel 43:2, *"His voice was like the sound of many waters."* (emphasis mine) Then again in Jeremiah 10:13 and 51:16 we see, *"When He utters His voice, there is a multitude of waters in the heavens."* (emphasis mine) Although other verses could be mentioned, we must assume from these that the waters above the firmament are words spoken by God coming from the place of His throne where He dwells. He is the beginning and the end; the voice of eternal life forever!

In Psalm 18:16-17, we see something different regarding the waters: *"He sent from above, He took me; He drew me out of many waters. He delivered me from my strong enemy, from those who hated me, for they were too strong for me."* Here we see the waters are bringing destruction from the enemy. In Psalm 104:6-9, we also see waters in a negative way: *"The waters stood above the mountains. At Your rebuke they fled; at the voice of Your thunder they hastened away. They went up over the mountains; they went down into the valleys, to the place which You founded for them."* Can we assume from these Scriptures that the waters above the heavens, where God dwells, are much different than the waters that are under the heavens, where man dwells. It would seem that the waters entail something much more than just words. The reason I believe this is because of the Scriptures that I am about to share. The first one is Revelation 8:8, which is the second trumpet judgment: *"Then the second angel sounded: and something like a great mountain burning with fire was thrown into the sea, and a third of the sea became blood."* The second Scripture is Revelation 15:3, which is the second bowl judgment: *"Then the second angel poured out his bowl on the sea, and it became blood as of a dead man."* In the trumpet judgment only a third of the creatures in the sea died; however, all the creatures in the sea died at the bowl judgment. We can look at these things as just natural disasters, but in context of Genesis 1 and the division of the waters, calling the waters below the firmament seas, we must conclude there is something much more than just natural disasters. This next verse confirms what I have just mentioned. In Revelation 21:1, John sees the new heaven and a new earth. What he sees next is very intriguing. *"Also there was no more sea."* The gathering together of the waters below the firmament was called seas and when all is accomplished in the end there is no more sea.

Note: Please bear with me through the next paragraphs.

Since God called the waters that were under the firmament seas, we proceed to Ezekiel 27, where the Lord addresses Tyre through a lamentation. I will only point out a few verses in this chapter. *"Now, son of man, take up a lamentation for Tyre, and say to Tyre, 'You who are situated at the entrance of sea . . . your borders are in the **midst of the seas** . . . You were filled and very glorious in the **midst of the seas**. Your oarsmen brought you into many waters, but the east wind broke you in the **midst of the seas** . . . the entire company which is in your midst, will fall into the **midst of the seas** on the day of your ruin. They will take up a lamentation, and lament for you: 'What city is like Tyre, destroyed in the **midst of*** *the sea?'* . . . *you are broken by the seas in the* ***depths of the waters.***" (emphasis mine) From all outward appearance this looks as if Tyre was destroyed in the sea. But seeing that God divided the waters and then called the waters under the firmament seas, we must assume that when it says *"in the midst of the seas"* it is referring to waters or people. Also as Revelation 17:1, 15 proclaims, *"I will show you the great harlot who sits on many waters . . . the waters which you saw . . . are peoples, multitudes, nations, and tongues."* Now we will look at Ezekiel 28 and his description of the prince of Tyre. *"Son of man, say to the prince of Tyre, Thus says the Lord God: Because your heart is lifted up, and you say,* ***'I am a god***, *I sit in the seat of gods, in the* ***midst of the seas***,*' yet* ***you are a man***, *and not a god, though you set your heart as the heart of a god. 'Because you have set your heart as the heart of a god, behold, therefore, I will bring strangers against you . . . and you shall die the death of the slain in the* ***midst of the seas***. *Will you still say before him who slays you, 'I am a god?' But* ***you shall be a man***, *and not a god."* (emphasis mine) We must observe that chapter 27 is speaking of Tyre and all of the activity that was transpiring within this city. Chapter 28 is addressing the prince of Tyre. In both of these chapters it speaks of their destruction in the midst of the seas. The city and the prince were in the midst of the seas when they fell. You will notice the prince said, *"I am a god!"* God said of the prince, ***"You are a man and not a god!"*** (emphasis mine) Then in Ezekiel 28:12-15, we see God addressing the king of Tyre, *"You* ***were*** *the seal of perfection . . . you* ***were*** *in Eden, the garden of God . . . you* ***were*** *the anointed cherub who covers . . . you* ***were*** *on the holy mountain of God . . . you* ***were*** *perfect in your ways from the day you were created,* ***till*** *iniquity was found in you."* (emphasis mine) This does not sound like God is addressing a man, but Satan. You will notice all of these statements are past tense. Satan, as the king of Tyre, became filled with violence and was cast out as a profane thing out of the mountain of God, as Ezekiel 28:16 describes. If the king of Tyre is Satan, then who is the prince of Tyre who says, *"I am a god"*, yet being a man?

Earlier in this chapter, we also spoke of idols and how Satan has used them throughout history to deceive mankind into the worship of something other than God Himself. I believe what is written in the book of Revelation is the, so to speak, "last ditch effort" of Satan to completely deceive mankind away from God. All that has been said up to this point will make sense within the context of these next verses. Turning to Revelation 13:1-4, we see the beast, *"Then I stood on the sand of the **sea**. And I saw a beast **rising up out of the sea**."* (Emphasis mine) It goes on to describe this beast as having ten horns, seven heads, and looking like a leopard, bear, and lion. What I would like to point out is that this beast came up out of the sea. He didn't come from the bottomless pit. He was a creation from the sea or the waters under the firmament, as described in Genesis 1. The waters under the firmament are the words or lifestyles of people and not God as we established earlier in Revelation 17:1, 15. This beast was calling himself a god (or God) as Revelation 13:5-8 says, *"He was given a mouth speaking great things and blasphemies. Then he opened his mouth in blasphemy against God . . . all who dwell on the earth will worship him, whose names have not been written in the Book of Life."* The second beast that comes out of the earth has power to deceive mankind and tells all who dwell on the earth to make an image; an image in the likeness of the beast that came out of the sea. This "image" speaks and causes those who do not worship this image to be killed. This image is not as the images of old. It has been granted the power to have breath or appear alive! As we saw of the prince of Tyre who said he was a god and was destroyed in the midst of the sea, so we see this beast coming out of the sea as a product of man's proclamations, deception, and self interest. What was God's image? *"Let us make man in our image according to our likeness."* (Genesis 1:26) Can you tell me what His image was like?

NAMES HAVE A NUMBER

"Then the Lord said to Moses: 'Number all the firstborn males of the children of Israel from a month old and above, and take the number of their names'" Numbers 3:40.

Each one of these firstborn males had a number. Their name was equal with their number. Each one's number was not anymore important then someone else's number. They all were firstborn males with a name and a number. This beast has a number. The number that he has is not anymore important than someone else's number, because he is just a man with a number as it says in Revelation 13:18, *"It is the number of a man. His number is 666."* The first beast (Revelation 13:1) and the second beast (Revelation 13:11) are one and the same. One of them is a man with a number and not with the eternal title: *"The First and the Last, the Beginning and the End, the Alpha and the Omega!"* He will present himself as having this title, but I'll let you in on a little secret: his days are numbered (three-and-one-half years). He has the number of a man (or the number of man). Man takes this number (the mark) on his hand or forehead. The mark is the number of his name. A number always represents a limited short time; since a number, once it is reached, has an end! In contrast, God is the Alpha and Omega, the Beginning and the End. He has no number, but He does have a name (above all names). He gives His Name to those who overcome. *"To him who overcomes . . ."* (Revelation 3:12) The marking on the hand or forehead was originally God's idea. We see in Exodus 13:9 and 16 that God introduces a remembrance of being delivered from Egypt. The unleavened bread and the redeeming of the first born son were to be as a sign on your hand and as a memorial between your eyes (or on your forehead). It was to recall that they belonged to God alone. The beast is the creation of man, but has been created and empowered by Satan who is only interested in the things of man as Jesus said concerning Satan in Matthew 16:23. He has the character of Satan as described by Jesus in John 10:10, *"The thief does not come except to steal, and to kill, and to destroy."* I see this character in those who take Allah for his word and follow him as did the disciples; taking Jesus for His word when they followed Him. They sold out everything to Him. When push comes to shove, most Muslims would side with all that the Qur'an says. These Muslim terrorist extremists take the Qur'an for what it says and then walk it out on this earth. That's why we see beheadings and the take over of nations. Their mandate is that all would worship Allah and all would live under Sharia law. This would be headed up by the 12th Imam or Mahdi, Islams messiah who is to come. My question would be, since Scripture indicates Israel being numbered several times, is this false messiah going to be a Jew because his name has a number? He will perform deceptive signs and wonders to deceive all people into worshipping an image that has literally come to life. So we see as in the parable of the wheat and tares, the enemy (Satan) sowed the tares and they were allowed to grow and develop until the end of the age in which they are then gathered and burned. We see this happen when the beast, the false prophet, and Satan are thrown into the lake of fire recorded at the end of the book of Revelation! They burn forever!

If we are to escape what is coming upon this earth, we must ask God to reveal any idol worship in our hearts. He must be our all consuming fire! Satan and his kingdom are developing along side the kingdom of God and we must discern between the two. The deception that is coming upon this earth at the present time is also sweeping "Christians" into darkness. How can we stand against the schemes that are coming if we can't stand for God at this present hour. You can fool yourself into thinking that you have time and that you can partake of this world to a certain point and not be effected, yet to open the door just a crack to a home invasion would end up disastrous. How can our lack of desire for God turn out any different? If you know the right things to do, no matter what the cost, you must do them. If you have to move away from friends that lead you into darkness, if you must literally run from evil, or shut yourself in for weeks at a time to get wisdom and discernment from God, then do it. Jesus is coming!

CHAPTER **12**

STANDING ON MOUNT ZION.

Revelation 14:1

Remember, in the breaking off of the seventh seal, we have seen Satan's fall (discussed in Chapter 10): the unraveling of Satan's kingdom and the manifestation of God's glory upon His people in the sign of the woman in labor (the salvation of the Jews). The sign of the dragon represents Satan's kingdom and the beginning of his demise. Revelation 13 is the description, in detail, of God's enemy and his followers who give allegiance to and worship God's enemy. In chapter 14 of Revelation, we see what God has desired from the beginning: a called people, an undistracted people, and a people that look just like Jesus. This has always been His desire! Satan has resisted and endeavored to destroy this completely. God's desire from the beginning was for man to rule over all of His creation. The temptation of Eve which led to the fall of both Adam and Eve was not a surprise to God. He was aware that these things would happen. Paul says in I Corinthians 2:7 when he was addressing the immature Corinthians concerning their dullness and carnality: *"But we speak the wisdom of God in a mystery, the hidden wisdom which God ordained before the ages."* God knew the outcome of the book of Revelation, all the while He created in Genesis chapter 1, establishing everything from "the light" to "the division of" according to His own mystery which He had ordained before hand! We must understand that God is never caught off guard. He has a plan that is indestructible. If I were God, I would want it all done immediately! God is most patient and so we see this patience also manifested in Jesus. As Hebrews declares in 2:6-8, *"What is man that you are mindful of him (or patient with him)?"* It goes on to proclaim how God has put all things in subjection under man's feet. As we look on man in this world, we don't see all things under his feet yet. This can be very disheartening and extremely discouraging to those who believe this. As wickedness increases in this world and seems to be completely out of control we must focus on this revelation. The Lord encourages us to have patience. Right in the middle of Revelation 13 where we see the manifestation of wickedness to its farthest extreme in the beasts ruling the earth, God has put an encouragement to His people, *"He who leads into captivity shall go into captivity; he who kills with the sword must be killed with the sword.* **Here is the patience and the faith of the saints**." (emphasis mine) This is in the context of saints still being on earth at this time. In the midst of all that is happening in the earth today with beheadings and the in-slavery (captivity) of people, we must have faith in God that He has a plan and has not abandoned His people. We must have patience with God when we don't see things happen as quickly as we would like.

This description of 144,000 must be noticed as it says in chapter 14:4, *"These were redeemed from among men, being first fruits to God and to the Lamb."* They are standing on Mount Zion with *the Lamb* and have eaten *the Lamb's* flesh and drank *the Lamb's* blood as Jesus proclaimed in John 6:54. They are seen as His example, which in no way belittles the rest of those who love *the Lamb*. They are **first** fruits, which means they are not the only ones! Remember that He said *"So the last will be first, and the first last."*

(Matthew 20:16) These are the last ones standing, so to speak. In the midst of all the wickedness manifested on the earth, God has brought forth what He has always desired: A people that carry His name on their foreheads! With these people He will put all enemies under His feet! I am not a first fruit, but I am one of His chosen ones; a saved Gentile just like most of us are. One of many who have emerged from out of darkness and wickedness and have washed their robe in the blood of *the Lamb*.

FIRST FRUITS: WHAT DO THEY LOOK LIKE?

"These are the ones who were not defiled with women, for they are virgins." Revelation 14:4

From the time of Genesis, we see Adam and Eve created for each other as husband and wife. God has established the union of a man and woman in marriage from the beginning. This is not only because of man's need, but it was a sign of the way our union should be with God. One man + one woman = marriage! From the time of Lamech, who was Cain's great, great, great grandson (who took for himself two wives in Genesis 4:19), we see man as out of control (or putting himself "in control" and forgetting God's rulership). As we see in Genesis 6:2, *"The sons of God saw the daughters of men, that they were beautiful; and they took wives for themselves of all whom they chose."* In other words, they were out of control with their sexual desires. I don't believe that these "sons of God" were demonic spirits that cohabitated with women. I believe they were men, the ones that came down through the lineage of Seth who is described in Genesis 4:25-26. (Either way you believe, we cannot be dogmatic, because Scripture is unclear on this subject. On that day we will probably all be surprised!) Here are some Scriptures to support what I believe. Seth was the righteous replacement for Abel. In Genesis 5:3, it is said of Seth that he is in the likeness of Adam, after his image. Adam was created in the image of God, so Seth was in that same image! He was a son of God and so it was for many generations until Noah. If angels (spirits created by God) impregnated earthly women, which resulted in Nephilim, then the virgin birth of Jesus was not so much of a miracle, but a response to evil. This would give credit to the devil for his miraculous activity making him equal with God. In Matthew 22:23-30, we see the

139

Sadducees questioning Jesus about the resurrection using a story of a woman who went through seven husbands that all died. They asked whose wife will she be in the resurrection? Jesus' response: *"you are mistaken, not knowing the Scriptures or the power of God. For in the resurrection, they neither marry nor are given in marriage, but are like angels in heaven."* Jesus just said that angels are sexless creations. They have no sex organs. It's hard for me to imagine sexless spirits impregnating women unless they have been given power as God has power. Angels were not created in the image of God like man, who was commanded to be fruitful and multiply and fill the earth. Angels are ministering spirits sent forth (Hebrews 1:14). We must remember there was another generation that was developing during this time; the lineage of Cain. Cain's generation was completely given over to earthly, fleshly desire. The last thing that was said of him, *"he went out from the presence of the Lord."* (Genesis 4:16) This must be noted: Two generations growing, developing side by side. One generation were men calling on the name of the Lord and the other generation had gone out from the presence of the Lord. Then as time went on, those of the lineage of Seth (sons of God) saw the daughters of men (lineage of Cain) and lusted after them. The results were mighty men, men of renown, known for their mighty (fleshly) acts. Just like Goliath, who was killed with one stone. Immediately after this the Lord said His Spirit would not abide with man forever, because man was flesh. It stands to reason that the women back then were called daughters of men because they came from man. Jesus called Himself the Son of Man, but that doesn't make Him just a flesh and blood man. He was born a son of man and the Son of God. Synonymously, Adam and Seth were in the image of God. Through the lineage leading up to Noah, they were quickly losing that image over to the flesh. His Spirit could not abide with a fleshly man. I believe what we see in these giants is an extreme manifestation of the flesh. Moses sent out ten spies who saw giants and came back trembling. Caleb was not trembling! (Numbers 13) After Israel's disobedience to enter the land, the Lord pointed out to Israel that Moab (Lot's descendents) had driven out Emim (a people tall as Anakim). Next God pointed out that the descendants of Esau had driven out the Horites and destroyed them. (Deuteronomy 2:9-12) Then it is described that Ammon (also Lot's descendent) as driving out and destroying

Zamzummin, a people great, numerous, and tall as the Anakim. Point being, if ungodly nations could destroy these giants, Israel would not have had a problem destroying them either, because God was with them. Then the Lord said in Genesis 6:3 that man's days would be one hundred and twenty years. I believe this does not speak of man's life span in years, but that there was a flood coming to destroy them all. He saw that the wickedness of man was great on the earth and that all of man's thoughts were for evil continually. None of us can be dogmatic about what we believe, because Scripture is unclear about this. But, it does make more sense to see it as the amount of years until man will begin multiplying and replenishing the earth. It seems that from the day God told Noah to build the ark until after the flood, the span would be one hundred and twenty years when man would begin to replenish the earth again. I'm not asking you to believe me. Just study the Bible for yourself.

After the flood things did not change. Imagine that! You would think after seeing mankind and all creation wiped out that man would live in fear and trembling before God. Yet immediately afterward Ham saw the nakedness of his father Noah. The point that should be made through all of this is that man has had a problem with women since the beginning! Then came Jesus Christ! He was tempted with all we are tempted with, but He was without sin. He remained a single man and had never married. So we see these 144,000 "first fruits" coming forth in the same likeness of Jesus. They are standing on Mt. Zion. In this present day of rampant porn and women in provocative dress, we see men who are undefiled and remain pure before God. They are not defiled with women! They are tempted, but have turned their heads to look away even from pre-puberty days and beyond! Were their hormones raging within them? YES! Do they live on another planet? NO! They are right in the midst of this world with all of its sensuousness, perverseness, nakedness, and filth. They follow *the Lamb* wherever He goes. Where He goes, they go. What He doesn't look at, they don't look at. What He doesn't give Himself over to is what they refrain from. What He loves is what they love. These men were spoken of in the prophets. Two prophets, Obadiah and Micah, prophesied of these men coming forth in the last days.

"Then saviors (or deliverers) *shall come to **Mount Zion** to judge the mountains of Esau, and the kingdom shall be the Lord's"* (Obadiah 21 - emphasis mine)

*"In that day, says the Lord, 'I will assemble the lame, I will gather the outcast and those whom I have afflicted; I will make the lame a remnant, and the outcast a strong nation; so the Lord will reign over them in **Mount Zion** from now on, even forever"*
(Micah 4:6-7 - emphasis mine)

These 144,000 men are outcasts. They are the lame of this world. They are the undesirable ones as far as Hollywood is concerned. They have no appeal to the masses. They are plain and unlovely. They are as Jesus was: *"He has no form or comeliness [royal, kingly pomp], that we should look at Him, and no beauty that we should desire Him. He was despised and rejected and forsaken by men, a Man of sorrows and pains, and acquainted with grief and sickness; and like One from Whom men hide their faces. He was despised, and we did not appreciate His worth or have any esteem for Him."* (Isaiah 53:2-3 - AMP). In this world we see great men, rich men, manly men, mighty men, important men, and highly desirable men; all being portrayed as models for us to emulate; yet who do we see standing on Mount Zion? *The Lamb* and with Him 144,000 first fruits; the lame and the outcasts of the earth having their Father's name on their foreheads. You might not be a first fruit, but you must have your Father's name written on your forehead!

MOUNT ZION

Have you ever asked the question, "Just what is Mount Zion?" Is it a real mountain? Is it Jerusalem? Take a walk through Scripture and discover this mystery. As we discover what and where Mount Zion is, we will begin to see more of a need in our life to be on this mountain. Mount Zion is like the narrow gate. Jesus said in Matthew 7:14 of the narrow gate: *"Narrow is the gate and difficult is the way which leads to life, and there are few who find it."* If you believe that Mount Zion is only just Jerusalem, then you live shortsighted. We will begin in I Chronicles 11:4-7 just after David was anointed king of Israel:

> *"And David and all Israel went to Jerusalem which is Jebus, where the Jebusites were, the inhabitants of the land. But the inhabitants of Jebus said to David,* **'You shall not come in here!'** **Nevertheless** *David took the stronghold of Zion (that is, the city of David). Then David dwelt in the stronghold; therefore they called it the City of David."*
> (emphasis mine)

Jerusalem (or Jebus) was a stronghold. David took this stronghold and set up his kingdom rulership within this city, so it was called the City of David. It used to be a stronghold of wickedness until David took it. Then Jebus was renamed Jerusalem (Zion) the City of David. The next Scripture, Isaiah 9:6-7, is key to seeing Zion. *"For unto us a Child is born, unto us a Son is given; and the government will be upon His shoulder. Of the increase of His government and peace there will be no end,* **upon the throne of David and over his kingdom, to order it and establish it with judgment and justice from that time forward, even forever."** (emphasis mine) The rulership of King David in Jerusalem was because of God and His government being established within this city.

In the next Scriptures we will see the development of Mount Zion, which has come forth through the cleansing and purging of Zion because of the invasion of Assyria whom God had raised up for this very purpose.

> *"Woe to Assyria the rod of My anger and the staff in whose hand is My indignation. I will send him against an ungodly nation. And against the people of My wrath I will give him charge, to seize the spoil, to take the prey, and to tread them down like the mire of the streets . . . As I have done to Samaria and her idols, shall I not do also to Jerusalem and her idols? Therefore it shall come to pass,* **when the Lord has performed all His work on Mount Zion** *and on Jerusalem, that He will say, 'I will punish the fruit of*

*the arrogant heart of the king of Assyria, and the glory of
his haughty looks."* (Isaiah 10:5-6, 11-12 - Emphasis mine)

*"Then Assyria shall fall by a sword not of man, and a
sword not of mankind shall devour him . . . says the Lord,
whose fire is in Zion and whose furnace is in Jerusalem."*
(Isaiah 31:8-9)

Zion was cleansed by God with His purging fire using
Assyria, and it was in Jerusalem that the furnace burned!

*"In that day the Branch of the Lord shall be beautiful
and glorious; and the fruit of the earth shall be excellent
and appealing for those of Israel who have escaped. And it
shall come to pass that he who is left in Zion and remains in
Jerusalem will be called holy---everyone who is recorded
among the living in Jerusalem. When the Lord has washed
away the filth of the daughters of Zion, and purged the
blood of Jerusalem from her midst, by the spirit of judgment
and by the spirit of burning, **then the Lord will create
above every dwelling place of Mount Zion**, and above her
assemblies, a cloud and smoke by day and a shining of a
flaming fire by night. For over all the glory there will be a
covering."* (Isaiah 4:2-5 - emphasis mine)

*"O God, why have You cast us off forever? Why does
Your anger smoke against the sheep of Your pasture?
Remember Your congregation, which You have purchased
of old, the tribe of Your inheritance, which You have
redeemed---**this Mount Zion where You have dwelt."***
(Psalm 74:1-2 - emphasis mine)

Mount Zion was and is the place where God dwells! It is the
place where God has been allowed to rule through His kingdom in
the hearts of men! Unfortunately man needs a spanking from God
every now and then in order to adjust his focus. Man's focus is
easily sidetracked. King David (a man after God's heart) established
Zion, the city of David, in Jerusalem as he ruled with righteousness.
God established Mount Zion in the hearts of men also starting in
Jerusalem. From the time of David, God allowed His fire to cleanse

144

and purge all filthiness from His people so that their focus would be on God only. Then He would establish His glory on them. David's reign did not start when Samuel anointed him king over the house of Judah. David's reign started when 400 distressed, discontented, and in debt men came to him when he was hiding from Saul. David became captain over these men. (1Samuel 22:1-2) Some of these, who were outcasts, went on to be some of David's most loyal and faithful mighty men. (1 Chronicles 11:10-47) God had captured David's heart and then through him, captured 400 men's hearts which grew into a great army of men captured by God's character and rulership. Again, as Isaiah 9:7 says, *"Of the increase of His* (Jesus) *government and peace there will be no end, upon the throne of David."* The city of David (Zion) had the reign of God within it through David reigning as king. God was very fond of David and made an everlasting covenant with David. Ezekiel was a prophet long after the death of David. In fact, Ezekiel prophesied after Jerusalem's destruction and during the Babylonian captivity which God had initiated and brought to pass because His people lost their focus on Him. Listen to what God says through Ezekiel concerning David and how God Himself will establish His kingdom in Zion:

"I will save My flock, and they shall no longer be a prey; and I will judge between sheep and sheep. I will establish one shepherd over them, and he shall feed them---My servant David. He shall feed them and be their shepherd. And I, the Lord, will be their God, and My servant, David, a prince among them; I, the Lord, have spoken." (Ezekiel 34:22-24)

"David, My servant shall be king over them, and they shall all have one shepherd; they shall also walk in My judgments and observe My statutes, and do them. Then they shall dwell in the land that I have given to Jacob My servant, where your fathers dwelt; and they shall dwell there; they, their children, and their children's children, forever and My servant David shall be their prince forever." (Ezekiel 37:24-25)

These Scriptures not only speak of David's reign over God's people forever, but also gives insight into what will be going on throughout eternity. It establishes that men will have positions in the kingdom according to their surrender and allowance of God's rulership and lordship over them. David's position will be shepherd and king over Israel. I was overwhelmed when I first saw these verses because it truly establishes a governmental reign, throughout eternity, that will be far beyond our comprehension. People do reign with Christ throughout eternity as Revelation 3:21 says, *"To him who overcomes I will grant to sit with Me on My throne, as I also overcame and sat down with My Father on His throne."* Also as Revelation 2:26 says, *"And he who overcomes, and keeps My works until the end, to him I will give power over the nations.*

David's reign in Jerusalem has been extended forever. The overcomer's reign over the nations will be forever as well. Since the Scriptures in Ezekiel speak of David's reign forever we must conclude that Mount Zion could also be equated with the New Jerusalem. The New Jerusalem is the eternal city of God that comes down out of heaven to be established on the earth forever (Revelation 21 and 22). When you read in Ezekiel 37 which establishes David being king and prince forever, you will notice immediately afterward in verses 26-28 that God's tabernacle and sanctuary are in their midst forever.

> *"Moreover I will make a covenant of peace with them, and it shall be an everlasting covenant with them; I will establish them and multiply them, and I will set My sanctuary in their midst forevermore. My tabernacle also shall be with them; indeed I will be their God, and they shall be My people. The nations also will know that I, the Lord, sanctify Israel, when My sanctuary is in their midst forevermore."*

Does this sound like Mount Zion or the New Jerusalem? Or both? Compare this in Ezekiel with Revelation 21 which describes the New Jerusalem.

"He carried me away in the Spirit to a great and high mountain (Mount Zion?) *and showed me the great city, the holy Jerusalem, descending out of heaven from God."* (21:10)

"I saw no temple in it for the Lord God Almighty and the Lamb are its temple. The city had no need of the sun or of the moon to shine in it, for the glory of God illuminated it. The Lamb is its light. And the nations of those who are saved shall walk in its light, and the kings of the earth bring their glory and honor into it. Its gates shall not be shut at all by day (there shall be no night there). And they shall bring the glory and the honor of the nations into it." (21:22-26)

SATAN DESIRES MOUNT ZION

As I've studied Mount Zion and desired to know more about the establishment of this place, I found something in Scripture that caused me to tremble. We have seen that Mount Zion is God's rulership over His people and that He is jealous over His inheritance with fiery jealousy not wanting any to perish. There is another jealousy that is seething in the shadows of darkness. It is a jealousy that is mostly unseen and undetected because of tremendous deception that lurks behind the scenes. If we don't have discernment in this day and age we will be swept into this dark undetected jealousy. What I am saying is Satan is jealous over Mount Zion as well and desires worship and adoration and rulership over her with great vehement desire. I believe this is why Israel is completely surrounded by Muslim nations that hate her with a great vehement hatred. Their desire is to destroy the Jews and make Jerusalem capital of all nations ruled by Islam. In these next verses you will see God's excitement over Mount Zion, but also the desire of Satan to be a part of it as well.

*"Great is the Lord, and greatly to be praised in the city of our God, **in His holy mountain**. Beautiful in elevation, the joy of the whole earth, is Mount Zion on the **sides of the***

north, the city of the great King. God is in her palaces; He is known as her refuge." (Psalm 48:1-3 - emphasis mine)

*"How you are fallen from heaven, O Lucifer, son of the morning! How you are cut down to the ground, you who weakened the nations! For you have said in your heart: 'I will ascend into heaven, I will exalt my throne above the stars of God; I will **also** sit **on the mount** of the congregation **on the farthest sides of the north**; I will ascend above the heights of the clouds, I will be like the Most High.'"* (Isaiah 14:12-14 - emphasis mine)

Listen carefully to what Ezekiel has to say in regard to Satan:

*"You were the seal of perfection, full of wisdom and perfect in beauty. You were in Eden, the garden of God . . . You were the anointed cherub who covers; I established you; **You were on the holy mountain** of God . . . **till** iniquity was found in you . . . and you sinned; therefore I cast you as a profane thing **out of the mountain of God."***
(Ezekiel 28:12-16 - emphasis mine)

We must take notice of Satan's desire to dwell in this holy place Mount Zion. If we are to remain untouched by Satan's schemes and dwell in God's holy mountain, we must not be dull of heart and lack understanding of God's word. Hebrews 5 says for us to be skilled in the word so that we may be sensitive and discern between what is good and what is evil. If we are still children needing milk and not solid food, then we will be unskilled. Peter exhorts each of us to grow in grace and the knowledge of Christ Jesus. Growing in the knowledge of Jesus is not just knowing about His death and resurrection. Those 144,000 who are standing on Mount Zion **follow the Lamb wherever He goes**. This is a picture of what growing should look like!

CHAPTER 13

FOR THE HOUR OF HIS JUDGMENT HAS COME

Revelation 14:7

This proclamation from Revelation 14:7 was made by an angel flying in the midst of heaven. This angel was preaching the gospel to every people group on the earth. He was exhorting all to fear God and give Him glory because "the hour" of His judgment had come. I thought I heard it said that His judgment begins to be released through the seals? Here it says long after the seals were broken and even after the trumpet judgments were sounded, that the hour of His judgment has come. We see a previously similar situation with an angel that is also flying through the midst of heaven in Revelation 8:13. This angel, who was also flying through the midst of heaven, was proclaiming with a loud voice, *"Woe, woe, woe to the inhabitants of the earth, because of the remaining blasts of the trumpet."* This angel was proclaiming a warning which came in the middle of the seven trumpet judgments. Notice that nothing was said about God's wrath being complete through these seven angels as it says in Revelation 15:1 concerning the seven last angels. In fact, the angel spoken of in chapter 9 (the fifth trumpet judgment) was only given a key to the pit and also certain restrictions in regard to the judgment that was released (9:4). Some angels were also released because they had been bound. Four angels who were bound at the river Euphrates (9:14) were released to kill a third of mankind. Why would angels have to be bound if they were holy angels? While they were bound they were being prepared to kill as it says in 9:15.

ONE MESSENGER---TWO MESSAGES

The angel in chapter 14 (flying in the midst of heaven) had the gospel to preach before the seven "last" plagues (bowls) in Revelation 15:1. The contrast between these proclamations is interesting. One speaks of woes and the other preaches the gospel. The proclamation of woes comes first, then the preaching of the gospel. This is interesting because in my thinking it would be reversed: Preaching the gospel and then comes the woes. You will also notice in Revelation 8:2, that John sees seven angels who "stand before God". They are *given* seven trumpets. Then in Revelation 15:1 John sees another sign: *"In heaven; great and marvelous: seven angels **having** the seven last plagues, for in them the wrath of God is complete."* (emphasis mine) We also see in Revelation 15:2-4, this marvelous sign: a sea of glass mingled with fire and those who have victory over the beast standing on it, singing. This sign indicates that victory has been won by the overcomer's because of the song they are singing: the song of Moses and the Lamb. Now God's wrath will complete His purposes.

Notice the contrast of the seven trumpet judgment angels that are "standing before God" at the breaking of the seventh seal, with the seven bowl judgment angels that "come out of the temple in heaven" (15:6). The bowl judgment angels description is exactly like the description of Jesus in Revelation 1:13, *"The Son of Man, clothed down to the feet and girded about the chest with a golden*

151

band." --- "Seven angels . . . clothed in pure bright linen, and having their chests girded with golden bands" (15:6). It would seem that these angels are much more connected to God then the trumpet angels. (Just an observation.) You will notice there is a marked difference between the results of these two groups of judgment angels. The trumpet angels' judgment results in destruction, torment, and death. The bowl angels' judgment results in sores, blood to drink, scorched with great heat, and darkness that produces pain. The difference being the way these judgments are administered. It's also noted in the bowl judgments that men blasphemed God because of these things; yet, just as in the trumpet judgments, men did not repent. Yes, in the midst of all these judgments, man continued in his selfish, lawless ways and did not turn from his sins! I must point out that God knew this ahead of time. He knew that man would not repent. If I was God and knew 2000 years before I was to pour out my judgments upon man, that man was not going to repent, I would simply say "Why bother waiting? I'll just judge them now!" (God is so very patient!)

Other differences between the two groups of angels:

Trumpet Judgment Angels	Bowl Judgment Angels
Given trumpets to sound	Given bowls to pour out
Come out at the opening of the seventh seal (which must be broken off the scroll)	Come out at the opening of the Temple in heaven
Come after smoke of incense rises to God	Come after the temple is filled with smoke from the glory of God and His power
Prepare themselves to sound	Commanded by a voice from the Temple to go pour out their bowls

Similarities: The trumpet angels were commissioned as another angel stands at the altar offering incense with the prayers of the saints (under the altar). One can't help but think that God's heart is so grieved by all the souls under the altar that He initiates and commissions them into judgment. Who was killing these souls? John saw a woman drunk with the blood of the saints and of the martyrs of Jesus. It also mentions this woman in Revelation 18:24

which says, *"And in her* (the harlot woman) *was found the blood of prophets and saints, and of all who were slain on the earth."* Also in Matthew 23:34-35, Jesus accuses religious leaders of this very same thing. *"I send you prophets, wise men, and scribes: some of them you will kill and crucify, and some of them you will scourge in your* ("Churches"- I'm sorry, slip of the keyboard) *synagogues and persecute from city to city, that on you may come all the righteous blood shed on the earth, from the blood of righteous Abel to the blood of Zechariah . . . whom you murdered between the temple and the altar."* So we see that it isn't just the evil, rebelliously wicked that kill saints, but the religious are culprits as well. We notice in Revelation 16:4-7, concerning the bowl judgment angels, that they address this very thing: *"Then the third angel poured out his bowl on the rivers and springs of water, and they became blood. And I heard the angel of the waters saying: 'You are righteous, O Lord, the One who is and who was and who is to be , because You have judged these things.* **For they have shed the blood of saints and prophets***, and You have given them blood to drink. For it is their just due'* (*they deserve it* - AMP). *And I heard another from the altar saying, 'Even so, Lord God Almighty, true and righteous are Your judgments.'"* (emphasis mine) There are two different people mentioned in these verses. One is from under the altar (a slain soul) and the other is entitled "they". Since blood was found in the harlot woman, we should assume that "they" means her or those "the woman" represents; which would be true, but in the first, fifth, and sixth bowl judgments, we see these judgments directly against those who worship the beast. Since the harlot woman is sitting on a scarlet beast and the beast carries her (Revelation 17:3,7) we are left with the fact that she worships the beast as well, along with the rest of those who dwell on the earth. What seems to be a focal point of God in the third bowl judgment is His people---those (under the altar) who are slain for simply trusting and believing in Jesus.

A very important observation must be made at this time. It is the place where the last seven angels of bowl judgment come from. It must be noticed in Revelation 15:5 what John had seen.

"After these things I looked, and behold, the temple of the tabernacle of the testimony in heaven was opened."

153

To a Gentile this has very little meaning because Jesus is our connection with God. He is our tabernacle of meeting. He is our testimony. To a Jew, or those who have made it a point to know these things, the opening of the temple tabernacle meant the intimate, face to face meeting place with God. The opening of the testimony is also very significant. In Exodus 25:21-22 it says, *"You shall put the mercy seat on top of the ark, and **in the ark you shall put the Testimony** that I will give you. **And there I will meet with you, and I will speak with you** . . . about everything which I will give you in commandment."* (emphasis mine)

THE TESTIMONY

God is getting ready to give them the Testimony. What is this Testimony? We will see what this Testimony is as we look at the book of Exodus. The setting is Moses on the mountain. It is recorded that he was on the mountain meeting with and hearing God's voice speak which begins in Exodus 24 and goes through 32:15. Exodus 31:18 shows this Testimony: *"And when He had made an end of speaking with him on Mount Sinai, He gave Moses two tablets of the Testimony, tablets of stone, written with the finger of God."* God had just given man his first Bible (The Testimony)! It was put in the ark, which represented His very presence dwelling with man. I hear many say that they love His presence; and rightly so. I say, you can't have His presence without His voice speaking. When He speaks His presence is there. His voice is always married to His presence. If you want an increase of His presence, you must hear His voice---and obey. It is out of these things (the temple of the tabernacle of the testimony) that the seven bowl angels come with judgment.

This is not the first time the temple in heaven was opened. We see back in Revelation 11:19 that the temple of God was opened in heaven, and the ark was seen in His temple. This happened after one-third of mankind was killed and then Jerusalem becoming center stage for the two prophets prophesying and the beast killing them, but then they being resurrected and caught up to heaven in the sight of their enemies. The temple being opened in heaven happened after the seventh trumpet sounded. Remember, in the days of the sounding of the seventh angel, the mystery of God would be finished (11:7). God is making it very plain that His presence will be upon the earth during this tribulation and the wrap-up stages. There is tremendous significance to the temple being opened just before the great sign of Jews being saved in Revelation 12. The dragon, endeavoring to put a halt to this, is enraged because he failed in his mission to stop this. Then he goes on to set up his beastly kingdom with his mark on the foreheads of his followers. In Revelation 14, God displays His people with His name on the foreheads of His followers. Army against army! Kingdom against kingdom! It is then that we see the hour of His judgment has come on Babylon (the false bride) who made all nations drink the wine of the wrath of her fornication. She lived a life of lawlessness and independence all the while claiming His name as her own. Those who worship the beast (the false messiah, savior) will also drink of this cup of wrath. But God has unfinished business at this point. He must reap the harvest before the bowl judgments (Revelation 14:14-16). The great winepress of His wrath is coming after the temple of the tabernacle of the testimony is opened in heaven and filled with smoke (the glory of God and His power). It is then that we see the bowl judgments poured out. You will notice they are poured out on the beast, his followers, and his kingdom as well as those described as "the harlot". The sixth bowl judgment is gathering all of the beast's kids together to a place called Armageddon (Revelation 16:16). I can't help but hear the heart beat of God sighing as He proclaims, *"It is done!"* at the seventh bowl judgment. The finality of that moment is very clear, yet we are left hanging in verse 16 of chapter 16. God is patiently planning the demise and utter destruction of the beast and his closely dedicated followers by gathering them together. I will pick-up on this after a few words about the harlot.

THE HARLOT

It says in verse 19 of chapter 16 that the great Babylon was remembered before God. This does not sound good. It says that God is to give her the cup of the wine of the fierceness of His wrath. What does the cup represent? Jeremiah expounds on this:

"For thus says the Lord God of Israel to me: 'Take this wine cup of fury from My hand, and cause all the nations, to whom I send you, to drink it. And they will drink and stagger and go mad because of the sword that I will send among them.' Then I took the cup from the Lord's hand, and made all the nations drink, to whom the Lord had sent me . . . Thus says the Lord of hosts: 'Behold, disaster shall go forth from nation to nation, and a great whirlwind shall be raised up from the farthest parts of the earth. And at that day the slain of the Lord shall be from one end of the earth even to the other end of the earth. They shall not be lamented, or gathered, or buried; they shall become refuse on the ground.' " (Jeremiah 25:15-33)

This Scripture from Jeremiah parallels with Revelation 18:6-8.:

"Her sins have reached to heaven, and God has remembered her iniquities. Render to her just as she rendered to you (My people), *and repay her double according to her works; in the cup which she has mixed, mix double for her. In the measure that she glorified herself and lived luxuriously, in the same measure give her torment and sorrow; for she says in her heart, 'I sit as queen, and am no widow, and will not see sorrow.' Therefore her plagues will come in one day---death and mourning and famine. And she will be utterly burned with fire, for strong is the Lord God who judges her."*

Why was the Lord's wrath so severe towards the harlot--- great Babylon? Because she looked at herself as the bride, yet she was full of the harlotry of her waywardness from God. She pursued luxury and riches and was led astray through deception. She was a stumbling block with a millstone around her neck (18:21). She corrupted the earth with her fornication against God (19:2). All the earth looked to her as a example of God's people, but just as the scribes and Pharisees were full of dead men's bones and appeared beautiful on the outside, she was full of lawlessness and hypocrisy. Throughout all of Scripture, Old Testament and New Testament, we

156

see the Lord's attitude and thoughts towards hypocrisy. I would like to make mention of something that Simeon prophesied concerning Jesus in Luke 2:35. He said that Jesus would be a sign which would be spoken against, and that the thoughts of many hearts would be revealed. I've found some references in the Old Testament where God reveals and exposes the thoughts of the heart. Isaiah 14:13 and 47:8-10 speaks of Lucifer and Babylon, and reveals the thoughts of their hearts. *"For you have said in your heart!"* He goes on to expose what they were thinking. We find this same statement again in Revelation 18:7 concerning the harlot bride. She says in her heart, *"I sit as queen, and am no widow, and will not see sorrow."* She has set herself up as the prize of God's heart, but in reality she is full of filth and the ways of the world. The very fact that she says she will not see sorrow exposes that she believes God will rescue her from what Jesus mentions in Matthew 24, Mark 13, and Luke 21 regarding the "beginning of sorrows". It is when man speaks openly his heart is revealed. When he speaks within his heart there is possibility for deception and only God knows what he says. Because this harlot carries this attitude in her heart, her plagues will come in one day. The entire chapter of Matthew 23 shows Jesus exposing the hearts of the scribes and Pharisees. He proclaims eight "woes" against them. He is most severe towards these, the religious leaders and the harlot bride of Revelation 17-18, because they are stumbling blocks and they corrupt and lead astray. He said in Mark 9:22, *"Whoever causes one of these little ones who believe in Me to stumble, it would be better for him if a millstone were hung around his neck, and he were thrown into the sea."* Jesus again expounds on this in the parable of the tares: *"Therefore as the tares* (darnel, weeds resembling wheat - AMP) *are gathered and burned in the fire, so it will be at the end of this age. The Son of Man will send out His angels, and they will gather out of His kingdom **all things that offend**, and **those who practice lawlessness**, and will cast them into the furnace of fire"* (Matthew 13:40-42 - emphasis mine) Notice Amplified calls these tares darnel or weeds that resemble wheat. In other words, they looked just like the real thing, but they were counterfeit. I expound more in detail concerning the harlot in my book, *The Counterfeit Woman*.

GATHERING OF THE BEAST'S KIDS

Picking up from where we left off at the bottom of page 139, the beast's kids were being gathered at a place called Armageddon. After one of the seven angels who had the seven bowls describes the great harlot's judgment (17:1-18:24), we see One who is Faithful and True sitting on a white horse (19:11). The armies in heaven following also on white horses. This is the direct response to those whom God has gathered together under Satan and his beasts. Notice in 19:17 that God prepares for this great victory by holding a supper. *"Then I saw an angel standing in the sun; and he cried with a loud voice, saying to all the birds that fly in the midst of heaven, 'Come and gather together for the **supper** of the great God.' "* (emphasis mine) There is a tremendously overwhelming confidence that this battle will be most victorious. The outcome of this event was a quick one. The beast, the kings, and their armies were gathered together (by God) to make war against Jesus and His army. Simply done---the beast was captured along with his prophet and then thrown (alive) into the lake of fire. Their armies were killed with the sword of Jesus' mouth and the guests (birds) were filled with their flesh.

CHAPTER 14

A WORD TO THE OVERCOMER
AND
THE HALF-HEARTED OVERCOMER

In Revelation chapters 2 and 3, Jesus gives seven promises to the overcomer. As you will see in reading these that God holds back nothing from the one who prepares and decides in his heart that he will overcome every obstacle within and outside of his life. We all have issues and those issues are what the Bible calls sin, or in some cases abominations! Please read each one carefully.

1) *"To him who overcomes, I will give to eat from the tree of life, which is in the midst of the Paradise of God."* (2:7)

2) *"He who overcomes shall not be hurt by the second death."* (2:11)

3) *"To him who overcomes I will give some of the hidden manna to eat. And I will give him a white stone, and on the stone a new name written which no one knows except him who receives it."* (2:17)

4) *"And he who overcomes, and keeps My works until the end, to him I will give power over the nations---'He shall rule them with a rod of iron; They shall be dashed to pieces like the potter's vessels'---as I also have received from My Father; and will give him the morning star."* (2:26-28)

5) *"He who overcomes shall be clothed in white garments, and I will not blot out his name from the Book of Life; but I will confess his name before My Father and before His angels."* (3:5)

6) *"He who overcomes, I will make him a pillar in the temple of My God, and he shall go out no more. I will write on him the name of My God and the name of the city of My God, the New Jerusalem, which comes down out of heaven from My God. And I will write on him My new name."* (3:12) (This is true even for the "no names" - the ones whose name means absolutely nothing to the rest of the world.)

7) *"To him who overcomes I will grant to sit with Me on My throne, as I also overcame and sat down with My Father on His throne."* (3:21)

God has very special rewards for those who come through the struggles of overcoming. As we see in Scripture, David himself had struggles. He had to overcome hatred towards Saul who was always trying to kill him. He had to overcome taking his own vengeance against Saul when he chose to only cut off the edge of Saul's robe instead of thrusting his spear through his body. David didn't look like much of an overcomer when he committed adultery with Bathsheba and then ordered her husband killed on the front line of battle. Yet, even in these things he was an overcomer, because he repented and confessed his sin before God. Being an overcomer doesn't mean you have reached perfection. It means you have the "Perfect One" perfecting an overcomer in you. We must learn how to gracefully fall on our face in repentance before God when we sin. So many today are compromising and glossing over their sin as if God winks at them saying it's ok!

So what happens to the one who does not overcome (or is a half-hearted overcomer)? We must look at Revelation 21:7-8 for the answer.

> *"He who overcomes shall inherit all things, and I will be his God and he shall be My son. But the cowardly, unbelieving, abominable, murderers. sexually immoral, sorcerers, idolaters, and all liars **shall have their part** in the lake which burns with fire and brimstone, which is the second death."* (Emphasis mine)

Let's take a look at each of these:

- Cowardly --- One who is half-hearted in his overcoming. A coward is one who backs down from being associated with Jesus when he is in the midst of unbelievers, yet will be ever so bold about his association with Jesus around believers.

- Unbelieving --- Unbelieving is like the unfaithful, evil servant (Matthew 24:48-49) who begins to beat his fellow servants and eat and drink with drunkards because he sees that his master has delayed his coming. He is also like the servant who didn't do business with the money given him by his master (Luke 19:20-23). He hid it away because he was believing his master to be a hard man. Yet we see the exact opposite with the first two servants who did His business. The master blessed them abundantly. This evil servant had an unbelieving heart.

- Abominable --- What does it look like when someone is abominable? Jesus explains this in Luke 16:14-15: *"Now the Pharisees, who were lovers of money, heard all these things, and they derided Him. And He said to them, 'You are those who justify yourselves before men, but God*

knows your hearts. For what is highly esteemed among men is an abomination in the sight of God.' "
We make ourselves abominable when we put pleasure and extreme honor and importance on things or others before God.

- Murderer --- Murder is equal to hatred. (Matthew 5:21-22) *"You shall not murder, and whoever murders will be in danger of judgment. But I say to you that whoever is angry with his brother shall be in danger of judgment."*

- Sexually Immoral --- I don't need to say anything about this except that marriage is a public agreement between a man and woman only and not a hidden shack-up experience.

- Sorcerer --- Offering to God what we think will move or appease Him when we know in our hearts it's like offering a pig on His altar. Example: Numbers 22:41-23:1-4 and 24:1: Balaam did not seek to use sorcery like he did when Balak took him to the high places of Baal where he proceeded to build seven altars and then offered rams on each altar to God in order to move God's heart. God will not share with demons!

- Idolaters --- What you talk about with excitement in your heart concerning things of the world is idolatry. We don't blatantly bow before carved images. We just bow before chrome and metal, wood and stone, comfort and ease, sports figures, rock and roll legends, and $$$!

- All Liars --- Notice it doesn't say "some liars". In other words all who lie or live a lie.

This list is under the title of believer (half-hearted overcomer)! They will have their part in the lake of fire, which is the second death. Notice in Revelation 20:14, it says, *"Then Death and Hades were cast into the lake of fire. This is the second death."* The second death is when Death and Hades are cast into the lake of fire. These have their part in this lake. It will touch them in various degrees, burning that which was not consecrated. You will notice in Revelation 20:4-6 that those who were beheaded for their witness to Jesus were resurrected first (verse 5, the first resurrection) and the second death had no power over them. The rest were not resurrected until after the thousand year reign. The point I want to make is that the second death had no power over them. So if these listed above have their part in the lake of fire (the second death) then we should take great pain and efforts to be a genuine overcomer.

I would also like to point out the second promise in the list of overcoming promises that are listed above. It says:
"He who overcomes will not be hurt by the second death
(the lake of fire)!"
Does this mean that he who doesn't overcome, or is half-hearted will be hurt by the second death? You must consider what this says!

It is vitally important to overcome in this day and age. We are constantly barraged with pictures and words coming from every direction demanding our attention, time, and loyalty. This has escalated extremely in the past 100 years or less. The things that our ancestors had to overcome have been multiplied thousands of times because of the internet and the operation of electricity. This tells me somethings up in these last days! You can be an overcomer! God knows the days we live in and has made provision for every lust and sin that we face. *The Lamb* has taken every perverted hateful thing that flows through our being and crucified us with Himself (*the slain Lamb*) to free us from them. He has also resurrected us with Himself (*the slain Lamb standing*) to live the God kind of life. Overcoming happens when a small choice is made --- turning away and turning towards. Prayer is important. Deliverance is important. Church is important. But none of these things can make us choose. They can help us, but the choice is in the moment we are encountered. David was encountered with temptation and in some things he made the right choice, in others he didn't. When he didn't, his response was to fall on his face repenting. This is the attitude of the overcomer who embraces *the slain Lamb standing*! They washed their robes in the *Lamb's* blood!

www.ingramcontent.com/pod-product-compliance
Lightning Source LLC
Chambersburg PA
CBHW061825040426
42447CB00012B/2813